CREATIVE INSPIRATIONS, LTD.
Birmingham, Alabama

From Darkness To Light

A Modern Guide To *Recapturing* Historical Riches
UNDERSTANDING AUCTIONS, COLLECTIBLES & ESTATE SALES

LaCHERYL CILLIE & YOLANDA WHITE POWELL

From Darkness To Light
A Modern Guide To *Recapturing* Historical Riches
UNDERSTANDING AUCTIONS, COLLECTIBLES & ESTATE SALES

Published by:

CREATIVE INSPIRATIONS, LTD.
Post Office Box 610296
Birmingham, Alabama 35201-0296 U.S.A.

All rights reserved. No part of this book may be reproduced or transmitted in any form or by any means electronic or mechanical, including photocopying, recording or by any information storage and retrieval system without written permission from the publisher, except for the inclusion of brief quotations in reviews or articles.

Printed in the United States of America
Cover and Interior Design by ALABASTER STUDIOS
Editorial Assistance by ANNE E. HOOKS
Photographs by LEON STOUDEMIRE AND LACHERYL CILLIE
Illustrations by DOLLECIA AUSTIN WHITE AND ZOE

Unless otherwise noted, all Scripture in this book are taken from the *New American Standard Bible*, © 1960, 1962, 1963, 1968, 1971, 1972, 1973, 1975, 1977 by The Lockman Foundation.

Quotes used on chapters 2-5, 7-8, & 10-17 were taken from *My Soul Looks Back, 'Lest I Forget: A Collection of Quotations By People Of Color,* Dorothy Winbush Riley, editor © 1991 by Winbush Publishing Company, Detroit, MI. Used by permission.

Every effort has been made to trace copyrights on the materials included in this book. If any copyrighted material has nevertheless been included without permission and due acknowledgement, proper credit will be inserted in future printings after notice has been received by the publisher.

Information contained herein is subject to change without notice. Extra effort has been made to provide our readers with the most accurate information available at the time of publication. Creative Inspirations, Ltd. assumes no responsibility for any difficulty resulting from a change in the cited information.

Copyright © 1997 by LaCheryl Cillie and Yolanda White Powell

Cillie, LaCheryl.
    From darkness to light : a modern guide to recapturing
        historical riches : understanding auctions, collectibles & estate
        sales / LaCheryl Cillie & Yolanda White Powell. — 1st ed.
    p. cm.
    Includes bibliographical references and index.
    Preassigned LCCN: 97-92326
    ISBN: 0-9658908-0-5
      1. Collectibles—Purchasing. 2. Antiques—Purchasing
        3. Estate sales—United States. 4. Auctions—United States
        I. Powell, Yolanda White. II. Title

    NK1125.C55 1998   745.1'0896073
                                  QBI97-40957

Dedication

To my grandmother, Beatrice Brinson, who raised me with tender loving care and the late John D. Brinson who assisted in the process.
- *LaCheryl*

In loving memory of my God-fearing grandparents,
the late Edward Julian White, Sr. and
Carmeta Francis Ferguson White
who left me with historical and spiritual riches
to pass on to my children.
- *Yolanda*

Acknowledgements

This book is truly a *creative inspiration* dictated from above and deposited into our hearts. We are extremely grateful to many people whose `labor of love' made all the various pieces fit together.

To Our Husbands & Children: WENDELL CILLIE, who put up with long project hours, mid-night runs to the post office and other general agitations. WILLIAM J. POWELL, our financial consultant, computer analyst, and business advisor. His hard work, sacrifice and "loving word pictures" navigated us through troubled waters. JOSEPH, JEREMY AND JORDAN POWELL, for their patience with Mom when longer hours were spent at the computer and less time on family meals. Their nightly prayers for "the book" was a great source of strength.

To Our Parents: BETTY PRESSLEY, LEON & JURALINE STOUDEMIRE, THOMAS & SHIRLEY WHITE, AND JEAN & BAXTER MACON, who formed a real cheerleading section, offering moral support and constant encouragement during difficult times. Their hard work with book sales, fundraising, and business development was a tremendous blessing.

To Our Creative Team: ANNE E. HOOKS AND DOLLECIA AUSTIN WHITE, were present from the beginning to help formulate a working title and develop subsequent chapters. Through their creative insights, illustrating talents, and editorial skills, we were able to stitch and weave this book into a beautiful tapestry.

To Professional Friends & Associates: KANDIE HARRIS, for taking the time-consuming job of transcribing dozens of handwritten notes into intelligible text, and for praying us through the enormous maze of publishing. ATTORNEY HELEN SHORES-LEE for legal and business support over the years and ATTORNEY SANDRA LEWIS for genuine friendship and personal inspiration. CAROLYNE BLOUNT of *about...time* MAGAZINE, who introduced us and brought us together on our first article to profile auctions and estate sales for the African-American community. VINCENT F. A. GOLPHIN, a seasoned editor and eternal friend who indirectly and unknowingly forced us to pour more of ourselves into the life of this project than we ever thought possible. ELIAS AND GAYNELLE HENDRIX for the liberal photographic use of their beautiful African art collection. ANGELINE STALLWORTH, who stopped by near the end of our writing woes and offered to complete those small, nagging pieces that we lacked the energy to do. CARL AND DARLENE MURRAY OF COLONIAL PRESS, who answered a zillion publishing questions and inspired our cover design. MARC LINDSEY OF EBSCO MEDIA, who came along at the right time and assisted us with professional layout options and expert printing services.

A Personal Note from LaCheryl: To my aunt, LOIS BRINSON, who shopped thrift stores and appreciated collectibles long before the rest of the family. To my long-time friends, PRIMA STEWART, JENNIFER WALKER AND DORIS GOODEN. Thanks for your help with Premier Estate and Auction Service. I am grateful for all of your support and inspiration over the years. A special thanks to TERRY WILLIAMS, OF TERRY WILLIAMS, INC. who helped me get into *Essence* magazine and share the message of 'auctioning' with the nation.

A Personal Note From Yolanda: To L. GLADYS BROWN, my faithful assistant, who willingly helped with household maintenance and office matters during this busy season. I appreciate the way you have kept me "prayed up" and "focused" on the bigger picture. To GWEN DEES AUSTIN AND THE LADIES OF NEW CITY CHURCH, who gave me a "Surprise Book Shower" when I considered myself "pregnant" with *From Darkness To Light* and unable to bring it to birth. Their acts of love and thoughtfulness helped me through a painstaking time. I am deeply grateful to those women who brought special gifts of prayer and encouragement.

Most of all, we give praise and honor to the LORDSHIP OF JESUS CHRIST, who gave us this collective vision and made it a living reality. Through Him *alone* "the darkness is passing away, and the true light is already shining." (I John 2:8)

Contents

Foreword 13
Preface 14
Introduction 16

    PART I: A MODERN PEOPLE RECAPTURING HISTORICAL RICHES

CHAPTER 1
Let's Go Back to the Old Landmark 21
An African-American Reflection of Tradition, Heritage & Wealth

CHAPTER 2
A Historical Stroll Down Craftsmanship Lane 25
A Highlight of African-American Artisans

    PART II: FIRST THINGS FIRST—UNDERSTANDING REAL VALUE

CHAPTER 3
Developing A Keen Eye for Value 43
*Valuation...Old vs. New...Furniture...Linens & Textiles
...Value Enemy #1: The Popularity Of Trendy Crap*

CHAPTER 4
Understanding the Tricks of the Trade 53
Provenance...Condition...Age...Rarity..Supply and Demand

    *PART III: YOU CAN DO IT! DECORATE YOUR HOME
    WITH ANTIQUES & COLLECTIBLES*

CHAPTER 5
Training Your Mind for Antique Greatness! 59
*What is an Antique?...Why Buy Antiques?
Let's Go Antiquing! Furniture Periods & Styles
...An Eccentric Thought: Blending Antiques With
African Motifs & Furnishings*

CHAPTER 6
Admiring & Appreciating Collectibles 77
*Glassware...Porcelain...Pottery...Linens...Jewelry
...Mixing Antiques & Collectibles with Modern Decor*

CHAPTER 7
Saving Ageless Items & Collecting Fadeless Finds 87
*"Don't Throw It Away!" - Items To Save In Changing Times
"Yes! Take That Home!" - Items To Buy & Collect*

CHAPTER 8
Color Me Black!..**99**
Putting A Spotlight on Black Collectibles

PART IV: WELCOME TO THE EXCITING WORLD OF AUCTIONS

CHAPTER 9
From Auction Block to Auction Gavel............................**109**
A Brief History of Auctions...Overcoming the Auction Block
...Auctioning As a Profession...State Auctioneer Licensing
Agencies

CHAPTER 10
Auction School 101:
An Introduction To A Fast-Paced World.........................**115**
Why Buy At Auction...Types of Auctions...How To Find
an Auction...Classifieds...Word of Mouth...Auction
Brochures...Publications... Government & Corporate
Auctions...Consignments: The Selling Advantage

CHAPTER 11
Advanced Training:
Developing Strategies for Auction..................................**123**
Nine Strategies for Buying At Auction

CHAPTER 12
Auction Day:
Maneuvering with Skill & Confidence............................**129**
The Auction Preview...Going To Auction

PART V: THE ESTATE SALE — ON YOUR MARK,
GET SET, READY, GO!

CHAPTER 13
Attending Estate Sale:
Early Bird Gets The Goods!..**137**
Estate Sales vs. Auction...Common Reasons For Estate Sales
...Where to Find Sales...Pre-Sales...Preparation Prior To Sale
...Attending An Estate Sale...Submitting Silent Bids...Payment
for Goods...Removal of Sale Items...A Note of Departure

CHAPTER 14
Getting Into The Sales Business....................................**143**
Should I Have A Sale?...A Word About Dealers and Collectors
...Hiring An Auctioneer or Tag Sales Conductor...Assessing Your
Estate

PART VI: TWO ROADS LESS TRAVELED—FREQUENTING THRIFT STORES & FLEA MARKETS

Chapter 15
Shameless Shopping In Stuffy Thrift Stores.....................*151*
Finding Stores...Eight Techniques For Successful Shopping

CHAPTER 16
Wheeling and Dealing At The Flea Market.......................*159*
The History of Flea Markets...Types of Merchandise ...Market Rules of Order...Buying, Bartering & Negotiating In the Marketplace...Selling Your Wares at Market

PART VII: FINAL HINTS & TIPS FOR THE SAVVY SHOPPER & COLLECTOR

CHAPTER 17
A Savvy Shopping & Collecting Summary........................*167*

PART VIII: MOVING FORWARD ON A LIGHTED PATH

CHAPTER 18
**Afterword:
A Practical Mandate for Families.....................................*173***
Special Keepsakes...Oral Traditions ...Spiritual Heritage...Material Inheritance

PART IX: THE APPENDIX - ESSENTIALS FOR THE JOURNEY

Decorative Resources *183*
Educational Mini Directory *185*
Antiques & Collectibles: Publications & Periodicals *187*
Where To Buy: Catalogs & Other Things............................. *189*
Auction Schools *191*
State Auctioneer Licensing Agencies................................... *192*
General Services Administration: Regional Mailing List *195*
Bibliography... *196*
Illustrated Glossary *198*
Index *211*
Meet The Authors *219*

Ignorance is the greatest Darkness
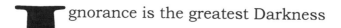

An Egyptian Proverb

Foreword

Collectibles and folk craft do more than carry on tradition - they mold and shape tradition for every generation. African-American craftsmen have made significant contributions to the aesthetic manipulation of natural materials like wrought iron, wood, fabric, and pottery for centuries. African-American artisans have also added important statements to the world of aesthetics, and have helped to define the relationship between abstraction and tension, form and function. Yet, at the same time, we have been able to illuminate shared community values and cultural history.

From Darkness To Light will help you understand the contributions African-Americans have made to artistic formation in this country. It will also inspire you to possess and maintain the creations of individuals who are the "keepers of the culture," individuals who are historic artists with penetrating aesthetic vision.

As you navigate through the exciting world of auctions, collectibles and estate sales, your depth perception will be increased. You will be able to spot the rare and the beautiful. More importantly, you will be inspired to pass these valuable pieces on to your children.

From Darkness To Light is a significant guide that bridges three important pieces for the African-American community: historic craftsmanship, non-traditional shopping techniques and family legacy. LaCheryl Cillie and Yolanda White Powell have designed something extremely artful and compelling in these pages. They have stitched aged-old textiles of the past with stylish fabrics from the present to adorn our children for the future. May the light shine brilliantly, your vision be enlarged and all your plans prosper!

Chris Clark
Quilter & Visionary Folk Artist
Birmingham, Alabama

Preface

From Darkness To Light: A Modern Guide To Recapturing Historical Riches - Understanding Auctions, Collectibles and Estate Sales is an intricately woven tapestry, combining distinct elements of the past, present and future. Like a giant quilt, this book has been stitched together using separate pieces of colorful fabric to create a wholistic rendering. Our desire is to unveil how 'family riches' (both material and spiritual) can be reclaimed and preserved for every succeeding generation. More than anything, we want you to see how richly blessed you really are!

Utilizing a unique format, this "how to" book fuses the philosophical with the practical, enabling you recapture historical riches in these modern times. *From Darkness to Light* is designed as a motivating guide and instructional manual to help you build family inheritance, establish family keepsakes and reconnect family ties from one generation to the next.

Many of us need only review our Grandmother's things with new insight. Others will appreciate "older" items stashed away in their own closets and cupboards, while others will create new "riches" with auction buys, estate sale purchases or thrift store finds. The means may differ, but the results are the same: *To recapture that which is past, bring it boldly into the present and preserve it for the future.*

We take this understanding from the Akan people of West Africa and apply the lessons of SANKOFA to our lives. SANKOFA means *to return to your past to fetch that which was lost and to move forward with it! From Darkness to Light* embodies this ageless wisdom.

Like our foremothers and fathers, we must be diligent to leave our children a legacy of posterity - a tangible reality that can be added to and passed on.

What are the historical riches that escape us in this present culture? What are we attempting to recapture anyway? Is it not the ceremonial tradition of "passing on" articles of value mixed with words of wisdom to our offspring? Is it not the official "changing of the guard", the "passing of the baton", the "conferring of the mantel" to those that will follow us? Indeed, it is the proverbial map that charts our way and puts us steps ahead in the race to leave this world better than we found it.

The wisdom of King Solomon confirms this necessity, "A good man leaves an inheritance to his children's children." (Proverbs 13:22) It takes great knowledge and planning to outfit our children with spiritual insight and financial stability in a complex and changing world. How prepared are our children to pass on the oral traditions of our families? Do they remember the hardships and victories of their foreparents? Do they know the names and profiles of the people from which they have emerged? What are the 'personal possessions' (great or small) that have woven the family together across time?

Whether it is an expensive silver spoon or an old penny jar, every family has a story or possession that must be preserved. Whether rich or poor, educated or blue collar, rural or urban – we need vision for the future. In this modern guide, we herald a legacy of *connectedness* - which is achieved through family keepsakes, oral traditions, spiritual heritage and material inheritance.

You will move *From Darkness To Light* as we stroll back in time and see the masterful craftsmanship of our ancestors; then sashay into the School of Value and understand how to assess the worth of various items; afterwards we will skip through a host of seminars on auctions, collectibles, and estate sales; followed by special trips to thrift stores and flea markets; finally, we will gracefully step into the reality of preserving a family heritage that will endure for all times. In the end, we will have journeyed effortlessly into the light on these intertwining subjects.

So, prepare for the journey of recapturing historical riches through applying the wisdom of the ages. The lessons of SANKOFA, coupled with the truths of the Scripture will not steer us wrong. We must return and remember. We must possess and preserve. Each of us must wisely lay a foundation for a future that we may never fully see. The pages of this guide will show you how! So, today come out of the darkness and into the marvelous light! Revisit, Recapture, Rebuild and Restore! Let the journey begin...

Yolanda White Powell

Introduction

As I look over my life, there have been many historical riches that have passed me by. I watched with little regard as my great-grandmothers' things including quilts, linens, glassware, and furniture were totally discarded by family members. We considered it junk for the pile. Many years later, I would begin a personal search to recapture some of these historical pieces. I can honestly testify that recapturing riches from the past has brought me great rewards and personal satisfaction. *From Darkness To Light* is a loving invitation to join me on this journey.

Over the last thirteen years of collecting antiques, I have developed an enormous passion for auctions and estate sales. There is an excitement that bubbles from deep within for such events. My entrance into these alternative sales arenas began in 1984. I was a poor college student, graduating from the historic Tuskegee Institute and eager to attend the School of Pharmacy at Samford University in Birmingham, Alabama. It was decided that I would live in an apartment off campus, so I definitely needed a bedroom suite. Furnishing my apartment presented a rude discovery.

I was frustrated after visiting one furniture store after another. Most of the quality bedroom suites I liked were priced between six and ten thousands dollars. Needless to say, this was out of my price range! In desperation, I combed the newspaper for garage and estate sales. After attending a few, I found the bedroom suite of my dreams! A four-piece cherry, Queen Anne poster bedroom suite for the unbelievable price of $900 (mattress included)! Today, our master bedroom is still adorned with this special suite. From that point, I began to frequent auctions and estate sales. My interest in antiques and collectibles would come much later.

Fortunately, my husband, Wendell grew up with an appreciation for antiques. During our courtship, I would visit his home and wonder why his mom filled their big beautiful house with such old furniture? As time passed, these items grew on me.

During a summer school stay at Tuskegee Institute, I used one of my future mother-in-law's antique beds. I believe a small spark of appreciation began at that time.

It appears that many circumstances like these, have been leading me to recapture an appreciation for my great-grandmother's things. I feel fortunate for that!

Inside *From Darkness To Light* you will become familiar with simple terms that describe the auction world and the estate sale process. Through a collective effort, Yolanda White Powell and I will demonstrate how auctions, collectibles and estate sales can benefit you in your search to recapture historical riches and fortify family heritage.

Quite honestly, I have found that anything known to man can be bought and sold in these non-traditional shopping arenas. You, too, will learn how thrift stores and flea markets can be the best places to shop for the most unique items at minimal cost! You will also gain helpful techniques used to find those "diamonds in the rough." Together, we will explore the world of antiques and collectibles – unveiling the "inside scoop" on how to gracefully maneuver in these circles. Also included are photographs of amazing things - we have purchased for just pennies! In the end, you will have a good idea of where to turn for information in these markets.

Furthermore, in the event that you are left with an estate to dispose of, its content will have new meaning. You will begin to understand value and recognize the tools to assess any items' worth. This is extremely important! Because there are antique dealers and collectors who would like to keep this information a secret.

I have been personally saddened by the pilferage that happens in communities of color (both urban and rural) by collectors who often flash a $20 bill for "historical riches" that are later sold for $2,000. It happens all too often.

From Darkness To Light is designed to shed light in all of these dark places. Like me, you will be surprised that many things that appear worthless actually have great value! As the light shines, you will behold many rare and beautiful treasures. Begin your search today! Recapture the historical riches that are all around you. Happy Hunting!

LaCheryl B. Cillie

PART I

A Modern People Recapturing Historical Riches

> "SANKOFA: Return to fetch that which was lost
> and to move forward with it."
> AKAN PEOPLE OF GHANA
> FROM THE ADINKRA

CHAPTER 1

LET'S GO BACK TO THE OLD LANDMARK!
An African-American Reflection of Tradition, Heritage & Wealth

Every generation looks back with a special fondness on certain aspects of their childhood days. Whether the setting was rural or urban – favorite memories are forever etched in the crevices of our mind. Most often, there are memories of extended family gatherings like the Friday-Night-Fish-Fry, Sunday Soon-As-Church-Is-Over Dinners and a host of birthday parties, graduation celebrations, wedding receptions and *after* funeral feasts.

Warm recollections provide a sturdy path upon which to move forward. Truly, our past is a powerful part of who we are! Even now, I can hear the continuous ringing of our doorbell, *O'Happy Day* blaring in the background and the cacophony of all-at-the-same-time conversation filling our living room like cigarette smoke. In quiet moments, I remember and smile.

How vividly I recall the scrumptious Southern delicacies that were prepared in my mother's small, hot kitchen; the feel of Aunt Lillian's freshly starched and ironed sheets; Aunt Irenes' plastic covered settee (that always made my legs sweat); the flea market what-nots that crowded Grandma Gladys' coffee table and the yummy jelly cake that was gracefully prepared each week by Grandma White. My memories are rich and refreshing.

Now, let's reminisce for a moment. Can you see that big potbelly stove, pure black skillet, or cast iron teakettle nestled in the kitchen of yesteryear? How about those perfectly folded handkerchiefs and cool cotton dresses of the 60's? Do you recall forgotten items like parasols, flour sacks, butter churns, dollies and weather vanes?

Remember the scrub board and clothesline (long before sculptured nails, washing machines or dryers)? When telephone numbers included letters (ours was TE-2723)? When older men drove one car during the week and maintained another for Sunday-Go-To-Meeting? When grown folks continually referred to their childhood friends as classmates? When homemade biscuits or baked sweet potatoes were as popular as hamburgers and french fries? When hand-churned ice cream and freshly baked teacakes were a regular dessert? Times have surely passed, but the pieces that define our family's existence must be preserved.

I occasionally serve as a contributing editor to *about...time* magazine, an upstate New York publication that has been "reflecting the African-American experience" for twenty-five years. In the February (1997) issue an article was written by Joan Marie Davis entitled, "Jelly Jars, Quilts & Flour Sacks." Joann shares her childhood memories of visits with her maternal grandparents, their family farm and life in their old log cabin in Shiloh, North Carolina. Through treasured memories she has returned to the "old landmark." Through her personal SANKOFA journey, she is helping to preserve her family's history.
"Most memorable for me are the products of my grandparent's creativity, resourcefulness, and innovativeness," she writes. My grandmother planted vegetable gardens and arranged flowerbeds near and around the cabin. Bushels of green beans, strawberries, corn and tomatoes were canned in Bell Jars. Flowers... were planted in flat bottom tin tubs, buckets, ceramic containers and clay pots. Jelly jars, whether empty or filled with edibles, served a variety of functions around the farm."

Joann's grandmother was also a talented seamstress that made most of the dresses, slacks, skirts, blouses and coats worn by family members. "Flour sacks, grain bags, old clothing, and 'store bought yard goods' were the materials out of which my grandmother fashioned clothing," she shares. "Two of my favorite outfits, as a child, were flour sacks dresses made by my grandmother." These dresses (which are more than 45 years old) were stored away and later given to Joann by her own mother.

Other significant items have been "passed down" to Joann, including her grandmother's quilts, intricately crocheted doilies, and lovely pieces of needlework.

During the past ten years, Joann has been recapturing much of her family's historical riches. "I have collected and restored many of the artifacts that were owned by my grandparents and great-grandparents. I have framed needlework, refinished furniture, restored quilts, repaired picture frames, collected jewelry, cleaned dishes and glassware," she writes. "My grandmother had the endearing quality of 'making something from nothing' and transforming ordinary items into treasured keepsakes."

This past summer a small group of women from our church attended The Great American Women's Get-A-Way in Monticello, Minnesota. This annual event brought together twenty-seven professional women from across the nation to discuss their need for spiritual awakening and personal growth. Attendees, Jean Whitlow and Gwen Austin both shared their experiences from a life-changing workshop entitled, "Grandmother's Pie Plate." During this time, women brought personal keepsakes, family heirlooms, wisdom stories, or inherited "strengths" or "affirmations" that had been passed down to them directly or indirectly from older family members.

The workshop facilitator shared with the women the special pie plate her Grandmother used to bake "love pies" for family and friends. Although her grandmother didn't have much money or lavish possessions to pass on, this pie plate represented her untiring love and never-ending commitment to her family.

Other family and friends across the country are returning to "the old landmark" in more direct ways. There is a trend among a vast population of Americans, toward building new lives on or near family homesteads. This is being sought in hopes of regaining that sense of "connectedness" which is often lost in our transient society.

My sister-in-law, Mia, is an excellent example. She is a single, cosmopolitan, and upwardly mobile professional living in Washington, D.C. Recently, she struggled with 'setting up house' on the 2.5 acres in Calvert County,

Maryland (about 35 miles outside of Washington, D.C.), where our family property was in jeopardy due to delinquent taxes. The other siblings were either too faraway or inhibited by financial strains to save our family inheritance. Fortunately, Mia was able and willing to step in and preserve the threatened homestead.

My deceased father-in-law had invested all he had into this brick ranch-style home in the country plains. His mother, Ophelia Clark Powell, had commissioned the construction of this family home before her untimely death. It was built on sprawling farmland that had been owned by generations of Clarks. With the homes of aging aunts and uncles closely nestled about, Mia could see the importance of relocating.

But, moving back to the family property would mean a slowed urban nightlife, an hour and a half commute, and the responsibility of homeownership. Yet, the wisdom of SANKOFA prevailed. After major renovations and modernized updates, Mia now owns a beautiful home that also serves as a country retreat. A few months ago, my husband and I were able to visit our sister, share in her accomplishments, and bask in the memories of what this homestead meant to those before us.

Mia's sacrifice enables our entire family to return to the 'old landmark' over and over again. A significant aspect of the Powell's inheritance has been preserved.

As we move into the 21st century, we must carry with us a richness of spirit and commitment to family. We must not sell off our *old* things and casually replace them with glittering new contraptions. Neither should we abandon the 'old landmark' in pursuit of temporary comfort zones. We must *always* embrace and acknowledge the strong cords that root, bind and connect us to our historical family system.

Like Joann, Mia and the many others who are recapturing an appreciation for our grandparent's things, we must foster a new vision for family preservation. When we hold fast to the age-old traditions, we are anchored and secure.

So, lets' go back to the 'old landmark' of commitment to family and preservation of riches. In the wisdom of SANKOFA, let us *return to fetch that which was lost and move forward with it.*

> *"People will not look forward to posterity, who have never looked back to their ancestors."*
> ALI MAZURI, C. 1985

CHAPTER 2

A HISTORICAL STROLL DOWN CRAFTSMANSHIP LANE
A Highlight On African-American Artisans

We begin our historical journey with a stroll down memory lane to highlight the excellence of African-American craftsmanship and to gain an appreciation for the artistic work of our foreparents.

These highlights will serve as an important prelude to subsequent discussions on antiques and collectibles.

Our history is so deep, wide and full that we have chosen only four artisans, from hundreds of thousands who have made significant contributions to American life and culture through an African motif.

Through the research of Dr. John Hope Franklin in *From Slavery To Freedom* we learn that by 1860 free men and women of color had a vast sampling of vocations, including that of craftsmen. Free black men performed jobs as engravers and photographers; while others were jewelers, architects, and lithographers. Almost every community had free African-American carpenters, brickmasons, shoemakers, seamstresses, cabinetmakers, and blacksmiths.

This small listing gives us a larger picture of the artisans and craftsmen who graced American history. Even through the hardships of slavery and second-class citizenship, African skills and methods of trade were somehow preserved. This survival is clearly seen in the lives of those we will spotlight on this historic stroll.

First, we will view the life and work of Thomas Day, a free black cabinetmaker from Milton, North Carolina; followed by Dave The Potter, as he was affectionately known (there is no last name), who was a literate slave, typesetter and renowned potter from Edgefield, South Carolina; then we will behold the historic Bible quilts of Harriet Powers from Athens, Georgia; and finally gaze upon the modern ornamental ironwork by Philip Simmons of Charleston, South Carolina - who is 85 and still involved in his craft through the training of others.

As we meet these artisans, we will be inspired to recapture the historical riches they have given both to America and their African-American descendants.

Thomas Day
(1801- 1861)
Free Black Cabinetmaker

The furniture carved and fashioned by Thomas Day holds a unique place in the field of American decorative arts. Our historical spotlight shines on this black artisan who successfully pursued his craft despite the harsh realities of Southern slavery.

Mary E. Lyons in her biographical work, *Master of Mahogany*, chronicles the life and work of Thomas Day. Her opening remarks gives us tremendous insights:

> "Tom Day's history is like a piece of furniture before it is finished. A few of the parts are complete and glide smoothly into place. Others are the results of guesswork, with only a rough fit. Some sections are missing altogether. Because the history of many nineteenth-century African-Americans was not written down, Tom's entire story may never be known. But we can assemble enough fragments to recreate the whole."

Tom Day was born free in Halifax County, Virginia in 1801. His mother, Morning Star Day, was indentured. In those days, free black children were taught to read and write. They were also taught a trade. During his apprenticeship, Tom learned to read wood like most folks learn to read books. He was introduced to the three methods of furniture design:

- mortise and tenon[1] joints for chairs
- panel construction for doors, and
- interlocking dovetails[2] for drawers.

These methods of joining wood together have been employed for thousands of years. Tom was able to utilize these timeless methods with creativity and precision.

In 1823, Tom moved to Milton, North Carolina. He was known as "a first rate workman, a remarkably sober, steady and industrious man...." Tom's excellent craftsmanship brought him much business. In addition to furniture, he made all kinds of items from wood such as cradles, coffins and fishing poles! Soon tobacco planters from throughout the Carolina region were hiring Tom to complete whole rooms of furniture for their homes.

According to Lyons, "the Greek Revival style that had been so popular in Europe finally arrived in the South

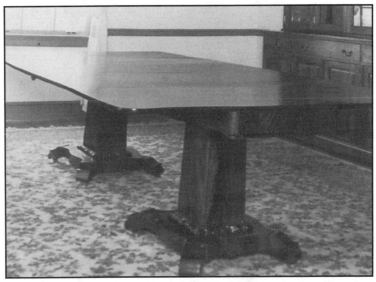

Thomas Day made this table supported by pillars, its scrolled feet are shaped like a column. *North Carolina State Archives, Raleigh, North Carolina.*

during the late 1830's. Tall white columns on the outside of plantation houses reminded the owners of ancient Greek temples. Matching woodwork and furniture on the inside made them [the planters] feel like kings and queens."

To follow this theme in his work, Tom built mantels, stairs, newel posts, cabinets and other pieces. He often traveled to the homes of rich planters, carefully measuring the height and length of each room. Paste-board miniatures of the furniture were made to show before actual construction.

Heralded as one of the best known of the antebellum craftsmen, Tom's furniture was highly sought by the richest clientele. David Reed, former governor of North Carolina admired Tom's craftsmanship and commissioned him to design a great deal of furniture for his family home. Many of these pieces are on public display in Raleigh at the North Carolina Museum of History.

Tom Day displayed great range and flexibility in his craft. He was able to design furniture after the Greek Revival style, as well as, incorporate African design techniques in his work. For example, the newel post he created for the Paschal house in Milton resembles a typical wooden stature from West Africa. Tom cut sharp angles into the wood to create the silhouette of a person. Then, he added a hint of body parts like the head, neck,

This Thomas Day bed has Empire style legs and a cottage-style headboard and footboard. He used four kinds of wood in its creation. *North Carolina State Archives, North Carolina.*

The newel post from a staircase of the Paschal house in Milton. *North Carolina State Archives, Raleigh, North Carolina*

breasts, belly, knees, feet and spine. "African sculptors often exaggerate some body parts to show their importance," writes Lyons. "The head is made large to represent the mind. Oversized feet and bent knees show calm strength and cool steadiness."

During the 1850's, Tom also sculpted a pair of twin faced African masks for a mantel, continuing the theme of West African art. While researching the life of Tom Day, we came across an antique secretary that was designed by this remarkable craftsman. To our absolute surprise, carved in the top panels of the furniture were SANKOFA patterns. It is stirring to think that something in Thomas Day cried out "Africa!" as he chiseled masterful wood creations in his workshop.

Thomas Day was indeed a "rare individual with superb skill." Through his unique blend of cabinetry and artistry, we can learn much about the design of fine furniture and the power of personal achievement.

Beautiful pieces of Thomas Day's furniture are on display at the North Carolina Museum of History, 2110 Blue Ridge Road, Raleigh, NC 27601, (919) 839-6262. Plan a family trip to the town of Milton, North Carolina where Tom's workshop is now a National Historic Landmark.

DAVE THE POTTER
Poetic Pottery Designer

Abner Landrum started one of the first pottery districts in Edgefield County, South Carolina during the early 1800's. But, his slave, Dave became "the most accomplished African-American potter of the period."

Dave was taught to read and write by Landrum and eventually put to work as a typesetter on one of his popular newspaper publications. When Landrum left the area for business pursuits, Dave became the new potter for Landrum's son-in-law, Lewis Miles of Miles Mill. As time progressed and fame ensued, this ordinary slave became known as "Dave the Potter" and his work distinguished itself as "Dave's Pottery."

It is apparent that Dave's typesetting training became the intriguing element in his new career. He often inscribed his works of pottery with rhymed couplets. These poetic pots stand as outstanding achievements in African-American folk craft.

Let's spotlight a few of the pottery pieces that reflect Dave's personal thoughts and artistic wisdom:

- Most of his rhymes were unique compositions like this, *"Made at Stoney Bluff/ For making lard enuff."*
- Other verses suggest possible storage use, *"Put every bit between/ Surely this jar will hold fourteen,"* referring to gallons.
- This rhyme joyfully cites a Biblical reference that Dave believed would allow early Christians to eat pork... *"Good for lard or holding fresh meat/ Blest we were when/ Peter saw the folded sheet."*
- Dave's composition skills were also directed toward monetary matters: *"This noble jar will hold 20 (gallons)/ fill it with silver then you will have plenty."*
- Dave was quite poetic on the growth and development of young females: *"a pretty little girl on the virge/ volca[n]ic mountain how they burge."*
- A jubilant message reveals a patriotic twist: *"The Fourth of July is surely come/ to sound the fife and beat the drum."*
- Concerning his own enslavement, he inscribed these

words: *"Dave belongs to Mr. Miles/wher[e] the oven bakes and the pot biles"*
- With true evangelistic style, Dave pens this rhyme concerning Christian salvation, *"This jar is made all of cross/if you don't repent you will be lost."* This couplet clearly reflects Dave's own religious convictions.

These poetic pots exemplify both individual achievement and African-American accomplishment. Dave's artistry represents a unique contribution to decorative arts in this country.

Dave the Potter's work consists primarily of very large open-mouth storage jars, usually about two feet high, with slab handles around the trim. One pot that Dave made could hold more than forty gallons. It is considered an extraordinary ceramic accomplishment by contemporary folk artists.

Not much is known about the life of Dave The Potter outside of his work. But his poetic verses reveal great strength of mind and character. Despite the shackles of

An original charcoal drawing of Dave's pottery. *Dollecia Austin White*

slavery, he was able to move freely in his craft. With an educated mind and a creative spirit, Dave was poised for artistic greatness.

Several pieces of Dave the Potter's original pots are collections of the Charleston Museum, 360 Meeting Street, Charleston, SC 29403-6297 (803) 722-2996

Harriet Powers
(1837-1911)
Quilter & Bible Storyteller

Harriet Powers is known to have sewn two pictorial quilts between 1886 and 1898. Both quilts beam with Biblical content and inspiration. The older quilt, in fact, is devoted entirely to scenes from the Holy Scriptures. Harriet's focus on Christian themes reveals the religious faith and Biblical world-view of many African-Americans during this time.

The 1886 Bible quilt displays several "Bible picture stories" from the Old Testament: Adam and Eve in their Garden paradise, Cain killing Abel, and Jacob's ladder dream and struggle with the angel. From the New Testament, Harriet depicts John baptizing Christ, the Last Supper, Judas and his thirty pieces of silver, and the Crucifixion. A host of colorful animals, crosses, small flowers, and sunbursts also fill the panels of this quilt.

The 1898 pictorial quilt features ten Biblical scenes and five panels concerning events of local history. The figures in the second quilt seem to "wave, walk, kneel, put hands on hips, and blow trumpets," writes Mary E. Lyons in *Stitching Stars: The Story Quilts of Harriet Powers*. "Stripes, polka dots, and other patterns also add movement to her pictures. The contrast of light and dark colors fills the quilt with life and power."

There are a few repeated Bible stories from the earlier quilt, however, the new stories include: Job praying for his enemies; Moses and the brazen serpent; Jonah being swallowed by a whale; the creation of two of every kind of animal (shown in three panels); and a depiction from the book of Revelations showing the angels of wrath with a seven-headed monster, the seven vials and the blood of fornications.

Four of the local history panels document environmental occurrences. The final panel is dedicated to rich people who know nothing of God, and a sow named Betts who ran five hundred miles from Georgia to Virginia.

Harriet's strong sense of morality shines through in this quilt. More than just a "story quilt," this second work is a personal statement of religious fervor coupled with a strong Biblical faith in God and commitment to His Holy Word.

Like a refreshing celebration of Christmas and Kwanzaa in late December, Harriets' quilts combine African decorative applications to reflect her Christian beliefs. The applique[3] and piece[4] quilts are the two types in which patterns of decoration most strongly reflect African influences. Harriet exclusively used the applique approach in both of her quilts.

According to John Michael Vlach, in *Afro-American Tradition in Decorative Arts*, "The applique' techniques used by Mrs. Powers are generally similar to methods known both in Europe and Africa. Textiles in Europe have been decorated with appliqued designs since the medieval periods and have been reported from Africa since the seventeenth century."

Born in Georgia in 1837, Harriet's quilting style and form may have been passed down from African ancestors who came to Georgia in the late eighteenth or early nineteenth century. "By that time," according to Phillip Curtin in *The Atlantic Slave Trade: A Census*, "most slaves

Dahomey print from the private collection of *Elias and Gaynelle Hendricks*.

Pictorial Quilt (1895-1898) by Harriet Powers, Athens, Georgia. Bequest of Maxim Karolik. Courtesy, Museum of Fine Arts, Boston.

were being imported from the Congo-Angola, although a steady trickle were still entering from West Africa into the Georgia region."

"This is important because the African traditions for appliqued textiles are heavily practiced by groups from that part of the continent," writes Vlach. "The presence of West African slaves in Georgia makes it possible, then, to link Mrs. Powers' quilts to African aesthetic systems."

Research by Vlach, Lyons and others on African textiles, reveals that Harriet Powers' pictorial quilts compare closely with African appliqued cloths in terms of function, technique, content, and style. When looking specifically at textiles from Dahomey (now Benin), West African, the comparison between artistic elements like the hand, and eye of God, the fish that swallowed Jonah and the snake in the garden, are striking in resemblance to Harriet's quilts.

We can only conclude that since Africans came to this country with extensive textile expertise, either directly or indirectly, these 'historic riches' were passed down to Harriet. She was then able to recapture the artistic forms of her ancestors and apply it in her quilting craft. Through Providential grace, her work has been preserved and passed on to all of us - with the connections of Christian faith and ancestral heritage still pulsating and strong. Without doubt, the Bible quilts of Harriet Powers are full of African influence and spiritual power.

Harriet Powers' personal explanation of her 1898 quilt. Paneled scenes should be viewed from top, left to right:

1. Job praying for his enemies. Job's crosses. Job's coffin.
2. The darkest day of May 19, 1780. The seven stars were seen 12.N.chickens to roost, and the trumpet were blown. The sun went off to a small spot and then to darkness.
3. The serpent lifted up by Moses and the women bringing their children to look upon it to be healed.
4. Adam and Eve in the garden. Eve tempted by the serpent. Adam's rib by which Eve was made. The sun and moon. God's all-seeing eye and God's merciful hand.
5. John baptizing Christ and the spirit of God descending and rested upon his shoulder like a dove.
6. Jonah cast over board of the ship and swallowed by a whale. Turtles.
7. God created two of every kind, male and female.
8. The falling of stars on Nov. 13, 1833. The people were frighten and thought that the end of time had come. God's hand staid the

stars. The varmints rushed to their beds.
9. Two of every kind of animals continued. Camels, elephants, "giraffes," lions, etc.
10. The angels of wrath and the seven vials. The blood of fornications. Seven headed beast and 10 horns which rose out of the water.
11. Cold Thursday, 10th of Feb. 1895. A woman frozen while at prayer. A woman frozen at a gateway. A man with a sack of meal frozen. Icicles formed from the breath of a mule. All blue birds killed. A man frozen at his jug of liquor.
12. The red light night of 1846. A man is tolling the bell to notify the people of the wonder. Women, children, and fowls frightened but God's merciful hand caused no harm to them.
13. Rich people who were taught nothing of God. Bob Johnson and Kate Bell of Virginia. They told their parents to stop the clock at one and tomorrow it would strike one and so it did. This was the signal that they had entered everlasting punishment. The independent hog that ran 500 miles from Ga. to Va. her name was Betts.
14. The creation of the animals continues.
15. The crucifixion of Christ between the two thieves. The sun went into darkness. Mary and Martha weeping at this feet. The blood and water run from his right side.

The 1886 quilt of Harriet Powers is on display at the historic Smithsonian Institute, Washington, D.C., (202) 357-1889.

Visit the Museum of Fine Arts Boston, 465 Huntington Avenue, Boston, Massachusetts 02115, (617) 267-9300 to see Harriet Power's 1898 quilt displayed in black and white on page 34.

Philip Simmons
(1912 - Present)
Master Craftsman of Ornamental Wrought Iron

The artistic work of Philip Simmons provides the best highlight of African-American influence on ornamental wrought iron. Today, Simmons is the "most celebrated of the Charleston ironworkers." He began his craft in 1924 under the tutelage of local blacksmith, Peter Simmons (no relation). The elder Simmons was an ex-slave whose father, Guy Simmons, had also been a blacksmith.

"The tradition carried on by Phillip Simmons has its genesis some time around 1825," writes John Michael Vlach, author of *Afro-American Tradition in Decorative Arts*. "The impact of this more than 150 years of ironworking is seen not only in Simmons' techniques and

Master Craftsman, Philip Simmons at 85. *Courtesy of Philip Simmons Foundation, Charleston, South Carolina* Photographed by Claire Y. Green

tools (some of which belonged to Guy Simmons) but also in his style of work." Through the legacy of these older men, Philip Simmons acquired the values, talents and skills that would sustain him throughout his long metalworking career.

For nearly sixty years, Simmons has fashioned more than two hundred decorative pieces of ornamental wrought iron including gates, fences, balconies and window grills. "The city of Charleston from end to end is truly decorated by his hand," cites a newsletter from the Philip Simmons Foundation.

Creating decorative wrought iron involves many intricate steps. The most important step in the creative process is the development of vision. Simmons says: "I have a tremendous vision, every so often it comes over me. I never dream about it. I get a tremendous vision. Every so often I'll visualize something. I never forget about.[5]"

This mental vision is key to ornamental ironwork. The craftsman must fully conceptualize his creation before any work begins. As a master craftsman, Philip Simmons relies heavily on his keen artistic sense to determine aesthetic beauty. The "feel" of the object is critical to his craft. With Simmons, changes are constant. As he successfully modifies a design, he shouts aloud "That's got it; that's the one, that's the one[6]," encouraging himself in his artistic discovery.

Plain old improvisation is the creative process of Philip Simmons. His works are constantly molded and shaped. This creativity is most evident in his lively approach to artifacts in his ornamental ironwork. His 1960 creation of the Snake Gate, reveals a true artisan at work:

"...on the first sight I made the snake – the

body. But the eye, I had to make several changes. Like the first, second, third, fourth time I placed the eye in the head of the snake, it looked at me. That was the snake.... The eye was complicated. You put the eye in it and you just see something that look like a dead snake. He looks dead. You know that's the important thing about the snake—it look alive. It's a rattlesnake. It's in a coil. He is ready to strike too."[7]

Detail of The Snake Gate by Philip Simmons, ca. 1960, Gadsden House, East Bay Street, Charleston, South Carolina. *Courtesy of Philip Simmons Foundation.* Photographed by Claire Y. Greene.

Simmon's snake represents the "first work in the long tradition of ornamental wrought iron in Charleston to feature a sculpture of an animal," writes Vlach. "It is a boldly curving serpent turned into four loops. It's head is broad and arrowlike with a protruding forked tongue. The tail shows seven rattles..."[8]

In addition to the snake, Simmons also hammered out an elegant egret and a spottail base. In 1976, Philip Simmons and two of his assistants were invited by the Smithsonian Institute to demonstrate their blacksmithing techniques and talents at the Festival of American Folklife in Washington, D.C. There they designed and constructed the Star and Fish Gate to reveal their unique talents to the nation. With innovative techniques and animated productions, Simmons has added creative adventure to modern ironworking. In 1982, the National Endowment for the Arts awarded Simmons its National Heritage Fellowship, the highest honor that the United States can bestow on a traditional artist.

The blacksmithing techniques of Philip Simmons represent a blend of cultural influences. Like Harriet Powers, Simmons has received a direct 'legacy of excellence' from his ancestors that he is liberally passing on.

In a recent telephone interview with Simmons, he shared his lifelong commitment to keep blacksmithing from becoming a lost art and the apprentices he has trained to follow in his footsteps. Simmons also talked passionately of his love for God "from whom all blessings flow" and his commitment to the children in his community. "Raw iron ain't worth nothin', you got to shape it for it to be something," Simmons revealed. "Same with a child, you got to make something of him.[9]"

Though retired, Simmons is a master craftsman that is still designing and teaching others the art of blacksmithing. In addition to gates, stair rails and balconies, Simmons has also designed knives, bar-be-cue grills, planters, candlesticks and most recently, book easels, coffee tables and night stands. Without doubt, Philip Simmons has contributed an exceptional mastery of wrought iron to our country that will stand the test of time and artistry.

For more information about Philip Simmons, contact the Philip Simmons Foundation, 91 Anson Street, Post Office Box 21585, Charleston, South Carolina 29413-1585, call (803) 723-8018 or visit his web page at www.philipsimmons.org. For an exciting tour of Charleston and the ornamental ironworks of Philip Simmons, contact Alphonzo Brown of Gulli Tours at (803) 763-7551.

Also look for a new book release entitled, *Catching the Fire: Philip Simmons, Blacksmith*, by Mary E. Lyons (Houghton-Mifflin Company, Boston, MA, 1997). Or pick up a recent edition of *Charleston Blacksmith: The Work of Philip Simmons*, by John Michael Vlach (The University of Georgia Press, Athens, Georgia, 1981).

Author's Note: We want to acknowledge the exceptional research and historical documentation that was available to us by Mary E. Lyons and Professor John Michael Vlach during the development of this chapter. A majority of our understanding about the life and work of these four artisans: Thomas Day, Dave The Potter, Harriet Powers and Philip Simmons, came from their superb literary and academic writings.

---

[1] Mortise and tendon are the joint created when a rectangular plug on one board fills a rectangular hole in another board.

[2] Dovetails are interlocking joint that connects two pieces of wood at right angles. Pins shaped like the tail of a dove are cut on the end of the board. Like pieces of a puzzle, they are then fitted into dovetail shaped cuts on the end of the other board.

[3] The applique' (or "patchwork") quilt have tops made of whole cloth to which varying forms and patterns have been cut from other cloth of contrasting color and applied or "stitched" down.

[4] The piece-work quilt joins together separate pieces of material in geometric patterns and borders.

[5] Vlach, John Michael, *Afro-American Tradition in Decorative Arts*. Cleveland, OH: The Cleveland Museum of Art, 1978, p.116.

[6] Ibid., p.117.

[7] Vlach, John Michael. *Charleston Blacksmith: The Work of Philip Simmons*, The University of Georgia Press, Athens, Georgia, 1981. p.55.

[8] Ibid., p.55.

[9] Ibid., p.143.

PART II

First Things First–Understanding Real Value

> *"Nobody buys pebbles which can be picked up on the beach, but diamonds sell high."*
> A. Phillip Randolph, 1919

CHAPTER 3

DEVELOPING A KEEN EYE FOR VALUE
Exploring The Tools of Valuation

Value is defined as something important, useful or highly desired. Items are considered valuable if they are significant to someone.

However, value varies from person to person. Along the way, we each develop our own system of value. The element of value begins in our emotions. It is reflected in the way things make us feel about ourselves, how we relate to others, and how others relate to us based on those things. In other words, we consider things valuable because they make us feel good. Things of value help us to set a standard of quality for our lives.

This kind of personal value can be best understood by looking at the following categories: intrinsic value, aesthetic value and functional value. You can focus your personal view of value through these three lenses:

- **Intrinsic Value:** Represents how an item makes us feel and its overall emotional appeal. Does it gratify or give pleasure?
- **Aesthetic Value:** Is it pretty? Do we enjoy looking at it? Do others enjoy looking at it too? Does it beautify or enhance a certain outfit, wall or corner?
- **Functional Value:** Is it useful? Does it give us a better quality of life? Will an essential function be provided as a result of this item?

When buying or selling, it becomes necessary to place

a monetary value on the items we love and admire. Valuation is an assessment tool for this process.

Valuation

Valuation is the process of assessing the monetary worth of an item. In the economy of life, we must examine personal property in appropriate terms. There are four basic assessment tools that serve us in terms of valuation. They are fair market value, liquidation value, replacement value and appraised value.

   a. **Fair Market Value** — is considered the price at which a willing buyer and a willing seller exchange merchandise without duress. Both parties are knowledgeable of and agreeable to the same price. Most people operate in the marketplace with this principle in mind.
   b. **Liquidation Value** — is applied where the seller is under duress and willing to resale far below the assessed fair market value. This often happens during times of divorce, relocation, aging limitations and bankruptcy. Liquidation value provides mutual benefits for both buyer and seller.
   c. **Replacement Value** — is that amount of money it will take to replace older items in the present market. For example, an item purchased thirty years ago for $20 could cost fifty dollars today. Replacement value must be given consideration when maneuvering in the world of antiques and collectibles.

Appraised Value — is the written or oral value assigned to an item by a professional who specializes in defining the worth of similar items based on quality, workmanship, age, desirability and supply. An appraised value is usually provided by a reputable dealer or appraiser.

As consumers, we can also use these general principles (of quality, workmanship, age, desirability and supply) when deciding what to pay for an item. While utilizing these principles, bear in mind that value is as individual as we are! There will *always* be differing opinions based on taste, style and personal preference.

Now that we have the School of Value down, let's review a few older items along with newer things to see how they compare.

Old vs. New

Although Americans have always loved reminders of the past, not everyone has a love for old things. Many times we have witnessed older items casually thrown out for new shining replacements. Many of our grandmothers even tossed older furnishings with little regard. This was done in part to the hard, economic conditions in which they lived. For years, there was no money to buy new furniture. So when the economy of the household improved, they went shopping for new items. What grandmothers and other relatives didn't realize was that they were making these well crafted pieces harder for later generations to obtain. The quality furnishings they threw out are now the rage!

Quality is the main reason many people prefer the old over the new. It is very expensive to manufacture high quality items, because most of these older items were hand-made. The cost to manufacture articles of furniture, as recent as 25 years ago, may be tripled the cost if replicated today. The reality of high cost has lead modern manufacturers to use cheaper materials.

Our appreciation for quality and the finer things in life is exhibited in the things by which we surround ourselves. Because of this, "old things" are now finding themselves in the arms of collectors. So before you toss out an item make sure you know what you have and how valuable it is.

Buying trends reveal a shift in communities across the country. Most of us seek the quality represented in older items. In general, many Americans want to recapture a sense of nostalgia (the ideals, feelings and materials from a different era or period). A traveling exhibition of the Smithsonian Institute came to our town recently, bearing historical items like, "Dorothy's red ruby shoes" from the *Wizard of Oz* and Abraham Lincoln's top hat. People were enthralled and excited about the memories of yesteryear.

Look at trendy eateries like Ruby Tuesdays, Dugan's, Thank God It's Friday (TGIF) and many others. Observe the walls and ceilings. Bingo! There are an assortment of vintage finds. Typically, you will see old pictures, toys, trucks, washboards, advertisements and signs. While waiting for meals, restaurant goers have a chance to reflect on familiar collectibles.

Old Magnolia Petroleum Company sign, advertising motor oils.

Now, drive over to the anchor stores at your favorite mall and check out the merchandise displays. Those Tommy Hilfiger pants look wonderful folded on antique tables. Major stores are also using old trunks, mannequins, books and beds to showcase their displays. Here, we see a love for old things being coupled with new merchandise.

Walk over to the jewelry counter and check out the current "1928" jewelry line. This popular jewelry is based largely on designs from that period. Again, we see an appreciation for older styles fueling new creativity. The designers of this jewelry line, while not able to stock the original pieces, have reproduced them as a reminder of the great workmanship of the past.

Top: *Bracelet of black glass (jet) beads, from 1920s to 1930s.*
Bottom: *Collectible sterling charm bracelet, from 1940s to 1970s.*

In the final analysis, there are plenty of new, valuable items being made today. You will, however, need to know what to look for and be willing to pay a hefty price once you find them.

Still, auctions, estate sales, thrift stores and flea markets provide the best opportunity to recapture "older goods." We'll show you how in upcoming chapters. For now, let's compare a few new items with their older counterparts. After careful examination, you should agree that older items are extremely durable and better crafted.

Furniture

So you need to buy furniture. Okay, let's go shopping! We'll start at a mid-range furniture store (which is probably where most of us will be). What do you see? Look at that nice dresser. Well, it looks cute. Let's pull out the drawers and examine them. How are they constructed? Are they dovetailed or nailed together? Would you believe that staples are used to hold the sides together? Staples! Not even nails! Three sides are made of wood, but there is no real beauty in the design. Now, let's look at the backside and bottom of the drawer. Chances are they are made of particle board (sawdust particles that have been pressed together). Given constant use or possible damage, this dresser might last four years. Then, guess what? It's back to the store for a new one! So, then, how should we assess its value? Functionally, it will have short-term usefulness. Aesthetically, it's new and nice, but not really pretty. Intrinsically, your pleasure will be short-lived! And don't even consider selling it!

Wash stand of German origin circa 1850-1860s. Dovetails of drawer.

On the other hand, let's look at an older, quality dresser made fifty to one hundred years ago. A quick examination proves it's *all* wood. Dovetails, not staples, are used to join pieces together. No pressed particle board here! This dresser will last fifty to one hundred *more* years! Even with constant use or damage, repairs can easily be made. The antique piece has intrinsic, aesthetic and functional value. Do you get the point? This historical, beautiful and useful dresser will serve outlast many of its owners. It is more economical and practical to buy quality-made furniture. Antique furniture is stylish and durable; and it always appreciates in value.

Above all, when it is finally time to pass on this dresser, as a material inheritance to the next generation, it will *still* be standing sturdy and strong for them to enjoy.

Linens and Textiles

The local linen mart is having a 'white sale.' How beautiful will those floral pillowcases and that stylish comforter made of polyester and cotton blend be after several washings? You thought you were getting a bargain. But, what about those little balls which develop over time? They make those sheets awfully itchy and hard to sleep on. Get the picture? You end up having to buy new bedding every so often – because of the fading quality.

Wouldn't you like to feel like a king or queen when you go to bed, rather than waking up in the middle of the night because your linen is scratchy and unbearable? One solution is to trade in your bargains for older sheets made of 100% cotton. Some of these sheets are embroidered with embroidery crocheted edges and rich dyes.

Linens of white work embroidery

Now, I'm sure you've been wondering, "Where can I purchase these linens?" Older sheets may be found at auctions and estate sales. While newer sheets, similar in quality, may be purchased at your finer departments stores (for a small mint) or closeout stores like Tuesday Morning or TJ Maxx. You should look for Egyptian or Supima cotton sheets with thread counts ranging from 250 to 750. The higher the thread count, the finer the texture. Once you sleep on these royal linens—trust me, you'll never go back to anything else!

Embroidery

This creative, handwork is a lost art. Embroidered needlepoint, cross-stitch, crochet, and knitting are beautiful to behold. Embroidery on sheets, pillowcases and spreads are also very appealing. Every piece has lasting value. Even after continuous washings, the colors remain rich and bright. These pieces still look wonderful after many years. Unfortunately, machines make most of the modern embroidery, and it's expensive too!

Pillow made from remnants of a Yo-Yo spread

Pottery & Porcelain

Pottery and porcelain have been around forever. These pieces were created out of our need for basic household items like cups, bowls and plates. Over time, pottery and porcelain have developed into an art form with rich colors and elaborate designs. Famous pottery designers you should look for would include Hull, Shawnee, McCoy, Rookwood, Weller, Watts and Red Wing.

McCoy pottery, pitcher & bowl set *McCoy pottery markings shown.*

Fine, older porcelain comes from different parts of the world. Sevres of France, Meissen of Germany and Nippon of Japan represent a few designers in the global marketplace. These companies provide hand-made and hand-painted porcelain that has been around some 100 years or more. The beautiful colors are stunning and eccentric. Each piece of porcelain possess a timeless beauty.

On the other hand, visit your local import store. Much of the porcelain is designed by decal work – where items have been plastered on. The individual handling and creative touches are missing. There are still good, valuable pieces of porcelain being manufactured today. However, they may be expensive to acquire.

Japanese porcelain set in Dragon pattern

Glass

All glass is not the same. Any way you view it, those 'two for a dollar' glasses at the local discount store lack the beauty and elegance of cut, pattern, pressed and hand-blown glass. The clarity of workmanship in fine glass designs are simply missing in cheaply made glassware; not to mention the bubbles that may be embarrassingly visible.

Overall, we can see that the value of older items simply does not compare to many modern variations. We want to fill our lives with quality pieces that can be passed on to our children. In order to do that, we must avoid trendy crap that is "here today and gone tomorrow."

Cut glass pitcher and glassware

Value Enemy #1: The Popularity Of Trendy Crap

In this section, you find modern or current items made within the last 10 to 20 years. It might be the latest trend in metal beds and furnishings, import furniture or cheap particle board furniture (which may appear as a quality piece with showroom lighting). However, ask yourself a few simple questions:
- How long will it last?
- Will the paint chip, or will the item fall apart in the next two years?

- If I had a sale would anyone actually buy it and for how much?
- Is it a fad or trend?
- Has it stood the test of time?
- Will it increase in value?
- Is it wood or wood grain?

Some of the trendy crap (or new stuff) certainly looks good today or at least it appears that way, but take a closer look. Do you feel a sense of connection to the person who made that piece? Is it something made by a machine? Did any quality craftsmanship go into the creation of the piece? It may be fashionable to own the latest trend in furnishings, but it certainly will not be around in 100 years. Owning trendy crap simply does not make good economic sense. Try to unload some of those items (from even as recent as 20 years ago) and see if it sells. After repeated use, it may not be usable for anyone else. We all use sofas, chairs, beds and tables everyday. So, it makes better sense to purchase the finest quality within a reasonable price range. Otherwise, we end up buying items over and over again.

In subsequent chapters, you will learn how to obtain quality furniture, without paying horrendous prices. These shopping techniques will alleviate the assumption that "I can't afford quality things." You can own well-crafted pieces—items that will appreciate in value.

So, don't be fooled by inferior materials and the substandard workmanship used in "trendy crap". These items will never stand the test of time!

On the other hand, quality furnishings usually hold their value and do not depreciate. So why spend money on items that are unpredictable? The things we own are an extension of our values. Therefore, we should buy items that will last, appreciate in value and bring continuous enjoyment.

In the next chapter we learn to overcome the tendency to buy "trendy crap" by learning the "tricks of the trade" for purchasing antiques, collectibles and other quality items.

> "When a thing is abundant, it is always cheap."
> TERTULLIAN

CHAPTER 4

UNDERSTANDING THE TRICKS OF THE TRADE
Examining the Elements that matter

Understanding value and the important differences between 'old and new' items provide a solid foundation for trading in the marketplace. But, there are still a few things you should consider before deciding to buy. They are the proverbial "tricks of the trade" that includes provenance, condition, age, rarity, supply and demand.

Provenance
Provenance has to do with who owned a piece or where it originates. Written documentation is extremely important unless there is someone living that can authenticate the piece and prove origin or ownership.

A good example would be the auction of Jackie Kennedy Onaasis' estate held earlier this year at Christie's (an exclusive auction house) in New York. The fair market value of a fake pair of pearls can range anywhere from $1.00 to $100. However, a pair of Jackie O's pearls sold for several times their actual value. The world went wild in an effort to own a piece of the First Lady of Camelot. Provenance prevailed! If those same pearls belonged to me, they would probably have sold at an auction or estate sale for pennies.

Provenance will also reflect in the *resale* of Princess Diana's seventy-nine formal gowns that were sold at a fundraising auction this past June. Christie's raised nearly 3 million dollars to benefit several of Princess Di's favorite charities. But, with her tragic death, many of the new owners of the gowns are taking this opportunity to 'cash-in' on their initial investment. According to a national media source, one man who brought a dress for $20,000 is seeking to resale at "ten times what was paid" at auction. He recently turned down an offer of $150,000.

Condition

Items need to be in a reasonable condition before they are purchased. The word *reasonable* actually means different things to different people. The terms that define *condition* are excellent, good, fair or poor. Use these terms to evaluate the quality of your goods:

Excellent: No work required. All pieces are present and the item can be used immediately without any additional costs or effort.

Good: Item may need a minimal amount of work. Perhaps some lemon oil or Old English solution can be used to bring out the original luster of older furnishings. For yellowing or stained linens a mixture of sodium perborate (found in most drugs stores) and water can be used to brighten and restore. Otherwise, if there are no missing parts or no apparent damage, you have a good buy on your hands.

Fair: Item needs a good amount of work. Parts may be missing, visible holes in textiles, or slight aspects of the items' value have decreased.

Poor: Extremely undesirable condition. Most of the item's aesthetic value has been diminished and the item is in need of tremendous repairs. One must decide if something has enough value to merit repairs and replacements. It might be easier to find a similar piece in better condition. Repairs however, influence the value of an item and may sometimes depreciate it's value. For example, a rare glass broken in major pieces will lose its value stacked against a newer unbroken glass. If that same glass needs a minor chip repaired it might still be very valuable.

Age

The older an item, the better it is! This is true for most items like furniture, cars, textiles, photographs, glass, porcelain, pottery, records and silver. Buyers and collectors attach a certain value to items that have significant age. On the contrary, the value of computers, VCR's, TV's, microwaves and other electronics, is based the latest technology. The newer an item, the better it is, because technology is constantly being enhanced.

As modern day consumers, we must maintain a balance between the appreciating craftsmanship of the past and the changing technology of the future.

Rarity

How common or rare is a piece? Can you find it everywhere? When people see it, do they say, "I haven't seen one like that before?" Rarity is descriptive of the survival and endurance of a piece. Many were made, but only a few survived. In general, rare items command more money.

Supply and Demand

The law of supply and demand simply states that when production levels (supply) are low, prices will be higher. If supply is abundant, demand will call for lower prices. When supply equals demand, prices are stable. The scarcity of goods leads to increasing demand and higher prices. On the contrary, a saturation of the market for a particular good results in a smaller demand and lower prices. The law of supply and demand is unaffected by quality.

Manufacturers today are not producing goods with the same skill and craftsmanship, as was done a century ago. This unfortunate circumstance generates an increasing demand for quality workmanship of durable goods.

All of these elements (provenance, condition, age, rarity, and supply and demand) help determine the value of an item given its immediate use, as well as future demand for that same item. The longer the durability of an item, the greater its value to you and others. Remember that we want to be able to pass on significant items to the next generation. A wise investment requires thorough research prior to purchasing. Provenance, condition, age and supply and demand are important "tricks of the trade."

We are now ready to educate our minds for antique greatness and classic collectibles!. So, put your thinking caps on!

PART III

*You Can Do It!
Decorate Your Home With
Antiques & Collectibles*

"To secure the blessings of liberty, we must secure the blessings of learning."
MARY FUTRELL, 1987

CHAPTER 5

TRAINING YOUR MIND FOR ANTIQUE GREATNESS!
Understanding the History of Furniture Design

Two working definitions lead our discussion of antiques. First, the legal definition (which is primarily used for import duties and taxes) defines antiques as those things made prior to 1830. The other definition (adopted by most collectors and dealers) consider items 100 or more years old as antiques. These definitions refer mostly to antique furniture. Cars are an exception to this rule. They become antique after only twenty (20) years. Semi-antique refers to items that are less than 100 years old; but are highly collectible. Examples of semi-antique would include pottery, porcelain, glassware, textiles, oriental rugs and jewelry.

Why Buy Antiques?
Antiques have stood the test of time. Certainly, cheaply made pieces were available in the past just like today. Yet the workmanship of the past has produced furniture to last! Most antiques beam with the skill and excellence of its craftsman. Each piece speaks to us of years gone by, of self-expression and unfading beauty. There are four good reasons to invest in antiques: appreciating value, durability, cost, and decorating flexibility.

Depreciation vs. Appreciation: Antiques do not depreciate in value like modern furniture. The cost of an antique can be slightly higher than a comparable piece purchased new. But, when purchased at auctions or estate sales, it is definitely cheaper to buyer an older piece than a newer counterpart of similar quality. When the time comes to sell and buy again, new furniture may result in a considerable loss. Antiques on the other hand, appreciate in value and may provide a handsome profit whenever sold.

Durability: The earliest furniture was made by hand. A cabinetmaker and his apprentices designed each piece with great skill. Furniture was well constructed and built to last, usually the best available woods. Furniture was initially designed for utility, but later evolved as an indication of wealth. Elaborate and ornate designs were employed for the rich. Americans enjoyed hand made pieces until the 1830's when furniture began to be mass-produced. The Industrial Revolution was instrumental in bringing about this change.

Cost: "A thing of beauty is a joy forever." Antique furniture comes in many styles and periods. There are enough variations and "examples of excellence" to please every taste and budget. However, cost is not the same as value! Poor quality is no bargain at any cost! Keep this in mind as you shop and acquire antiques for your family. Above all, be willing to pay the cost for pieces that can be passed down to your children.

Decorating Flexibility: Antique pieces can be extremely versatile. They can be moved from room to room to enhance decorating plans. Antiques can also be combined with modern pieces to add an elegant flair to any room. Unlike modern suites of furniture, you can buy individual pieces of antique furnishings at different times, based on your pocket allowance.

Let's Go *Antiquing!*
Furniture Periods and Styles

Furniture can be divided into major periods and styles. A period is the term used to define the original time frame of a popular design. Style refers to furniture pieces that were designed based on an earlier period. The following are brief summaries of important periods and styles.

Colonial (1620-1776)

The Jacobean or William and Mary furniture were made while America was only a few English colonies. This furniture was simple, plain, and better suited for the "everyday" needs of the settlers. This furniture includes Brewster and Carver chairs, hutch tables, slatback chairs, Welsh cupboards, trestle tables, gateleg tables and board chests.

This furniture was bulky, heavy in appearance, and very uncomfortable. Few of these historic pieces actually survived. Many natural woods were used including ash, cherry, hickory, maple, oak and pine. The majority of Colonial pieces found today are reproductions.

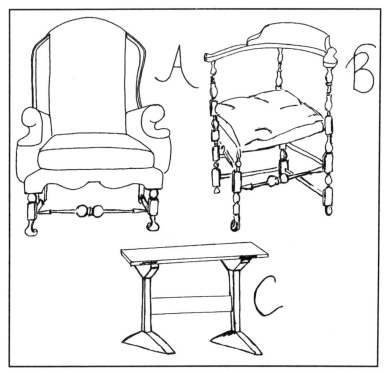

COLONIAL: **A)** *Wing-back (easy) chair,* **B)** *Corner Chair,* **C)** *Trestle Table*

Queen Anne (1702-1760)

Queen Anne furniture is still very popular today. This style transformed the bulky furniture of the earlier period into very nice, sleek lines. The "S" curve or "cyma curve" taken from the Greeks (meaning "double curve") characterizes Queen Anne furniture. The cabriole leg, which is the predominant characteristic of this style, curves outward at the knee and then tapers at the ankle. The foot may be padded, slippered, or occasionally ball and claw.

During the Queen Anne period, the plain colonial style became exquisite, tall and stately. Even the fully upholstered chair" was introduced for the first time in the form of the comfortable wing chair."

Shells are the central motif and carving ornament of the Queen Anne style. These shells appear in abundance in the knees of the cabriole legs, the backs of chairs, in middle drawers and upon the aprons of cabinet pieces.

The surfaces were plain for the most part in order to not detract from the "line of beauty." Walnut was the most predominant wood.

This style is still being reproduced today due to its continued popularity and comfort. Original pieces of this period can still be found, but are very expensive.

Chippendale (1750-1785)

Thomas Chippendale was an English cabinetmaker who lived from 1714 to 1779. His style consisted of elaborate carvings with the free use of curves.

The ball and claw, club, web and drake feet works are the main characteristics of this style. It is very similar to Queen Anne, except that the curved leg now has the ball and claw foot. Other designs used were a straight leg called the *Marlborough*. Bracket feet were used on furniture pieces, such as desks and chest of drawers. Carved ladder back chairs and fret work are also indications of this period.

Because Chinese designs were en vogue, Chippendale used a great deal of oriental motifs. Popular carving designs include swags, shells, and knotted ribbons.

Chippendale furniture was beautifully designed and crafted using mahogany wood. Although period pieces can be found today, they are very expensive. However, many reproductions are still available.

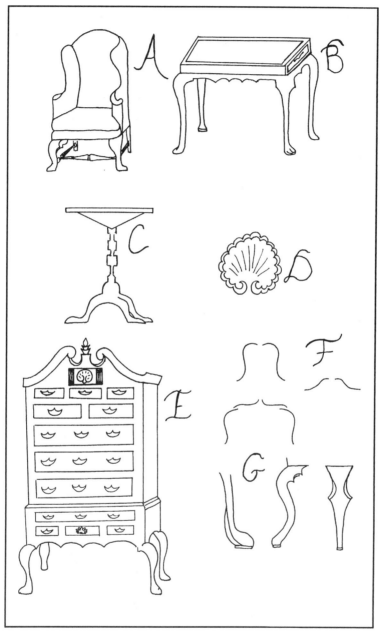

QUEEN ANNE: A) *Wing-chair* **B)** *Tea table* **C)** *Tripod table* **D)** *Shell ornament* **E)** *Highboy* **F)** *Cyma curves* **G)** *Cabriole legs with club or pad foot.*

CHIPPENDALE: A) *Chair with Marlborough legs* **B)** *Chair with shell ornament, fretwork, and ball and claw feet.* **C)** *Sofa with Marlborough legs and hump-back* **D)** *Secretary with bracket feet* **E)** *Bracket feet* **F)** *Cabriole leg with ball and claw foot* **G)** *drake foot.*

Hepplewhite (1770-1790)
At the end of the eighteenth century around 1780, the Hepplewhite period began with the designs of George Hepplewhite. Two brothers, Robert and James Adams, were major architects and furniture designers during this period. They had a tremendous influence on Hepplewhite's furniture designs.

Hepplewhite is characterized by lightweight furniture with straight leg forms. Serpentine fronts, refined curves, excellent inlay work and shield-back chairs, distinguish this style. Ovals, urns and garlands represent popular woodcarvings. Spade feet were also a favorite, and usually had square tapered legs.

Hepplewhite's chairs were not very strong structurally. They were however, original designs that included the shield backs, interlocking hearts and oval backs. Upholstery was carried down over the frame and finished with ornamental upholstery tacks. Sideboards (or buffets) became popular during this period. Mahogany was the wood of choice. Rare woods such as satinwood, tulipwood and violetwood were used for inlays. Many pieces have been reproduced and remain available today.

Sheraton (1750-1815)
Thomas Sheraton (1705-1806) was an English cabinetmaker, designer, publisher and preacher. His designs were widely accepted and they greatly influenced American furniture.

Sheraton's style is characterized by square, straight-lined, solidly constructed furniture. Sheraton's style consisted of round tapered legs with reeding of spiraling turnings. Mahogany was the popular wood of the day.

Hepplewhite and Sheraton styles are extremely similar. It is often difficult to tell them apart. Furniture historians conclude, "what we call Sheraton in America is often called Hepplewhite in England." This style remains popular today. Many pieces have been reproduced and are still available.

Duncan Phyfe (1795-1856)
Duncan Phyfe was an English cabinetmaker, who adapted and interpreted existing furniture styles. Personal adaptations were added to late Sheraton and early Empire styles.

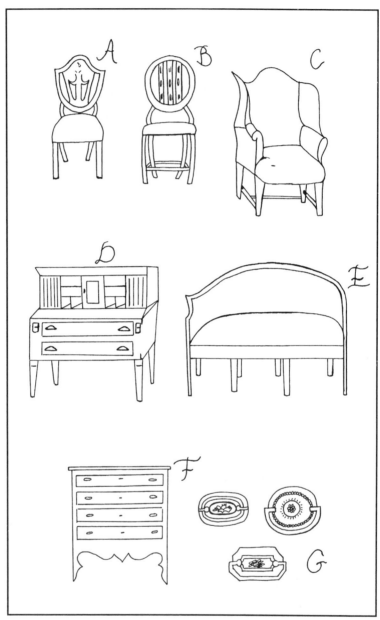

HEPPLEWHITE: A, B) *Side chairs with shield backs* **C)** *Wing chair* **D)** *Desk* **E)** *Sofa* **F)** *Chest of Drawers* **G)** *Brasses—*
Continued on page 76

SHERATON & DUNCAN PHYFE: A) *Sheraton chair* B) *Drum table* C) *Tapered Sheraton legs* D) *Duncan Phyfe chair* E) *Duncan Phyfe sofa*

Empire (1815-1840)

The American Empire (pronounced um-peer) was a heavy and massive furniture. The more expensive pieces are carved and contain motifs derived from nature, architecture and Greek mythology. These motifs include serpents, cornucopia, and other Greek designs. Acanthus leaves, pineapples, animal paw feet, and lion head brasses can also be found. Mahogany was used alone or in combination with veneers (where a thin piece of wood is glued on top of another piece of wood). Common furniture pieces include, sleigh beds, sofas with winged feet, and bear claw feet, as well as, heavy tables with and pineapple pedestals. Fret work and curly Q's were popular designs. Everything was flamboyant and frilly. These pieces can be found in many households today.

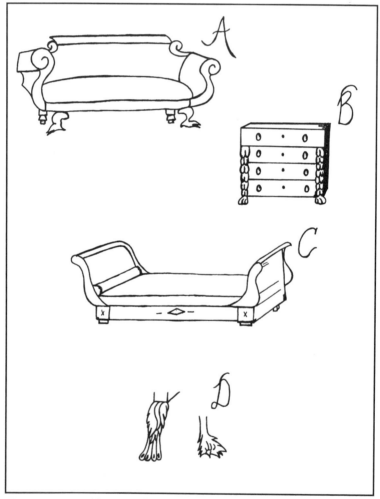

EMPIRE: A) *Sofa* **B)** *Chest of drawers with paw feet* **C)** *Sleigh bed* **D)** *Carved animal feet*

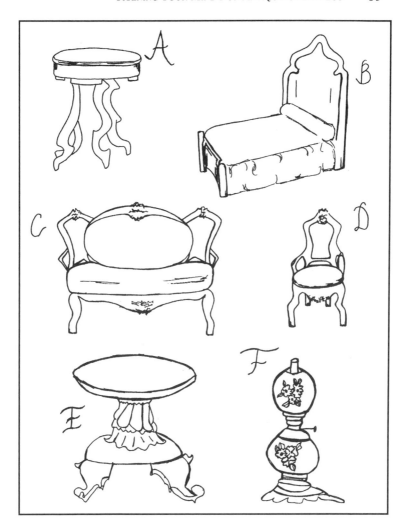

VICTORIAN: **A)** *Marble-top table* **B)** *High-back bed* **C)** *Sofa* **D)** *Side-chair* **E)** *Table* **F)** *Gone-with-the-wind lamp*

Victorian (1840-1900)

Queen Victoria served on the throne of England from 1837-1901. The furniture fashioned at this time was named after her. The Victorian period can be characterized by several styles including Gothic, Victorian, Rococo, Renaissance and Eastlake.

Gothic Style: Straight lines characterize this style. Architectural motifs founded on the great European Cathedrals built during the fourteenth century predominate this furniture. There are arches, trefoils, quatrefoils, and rosettes. This furniture is not as popular or abundant the other Victorian styles.

Victorian Rococo: This style is very popular, intermingling shells, grapes and foliage into flowing curves and rocky lines. This furniture is very popular and still being reproduced today. Mahogany is the predominant wood.

Victorian Renaissance: Furniture from the Victorian Renaissance is heavily decorated. The cartouche motif was used as the center decoration on chairs, beds, mirrors sideboards (or buffets). Mahogany and walnut were the predominant woods. This furniture is plentiful today.

Victorian Eastlake: English architect, Charles Locke Eastlake inspired this style. Main characteristics like burl wood or veneered panels appear on drawer fronts, cupboard doors and chair backs. An incised motif would be carved into pure wood, as opposed to using veneer (thin) panels. Original pieces of Eastlake were made of mahogany and walnut. They are still available today. Reproductions are also plentiful and affordable.

General Characteristics of the Victorian Period: Marble tops were frequently used on tables, chest, and commodes.Walnut and rosewood were the most common woods used. Furniture items included wash stands, hall trees, and massive beds. Metal furniture included ice cream chairs and tables, as well as, brass and iron beds.

Art Nouveau (1890's)

Art Nouveau is associated with flowing lines and curves. This style was popular in Europe during the 1870's and later spread to America. Famous craftsman during this period would include Philip Handel, Lewis Comfort Tiffany and E'mile Galle'. This style was most often used in production of metalwork, jewelry, art glass, graphics, lamps, and brass beds. This style of furniture is not reproduced much, due to a low demand for it. However, there is still great demand for the decorative pieces.

VICTORIA GOTHIC, ROCOCO, RENAISSANCE & EASTLAKE:
A) *Gothic chair* **B)** *Bohemian glass compote* **C)** *Rococo chair*
D) *Renaissance chair and chest of drawers* **E)** *Eastlake chair and bed*

Golden Oak (1890's - 1920's)

With Golden Oak, the wood grain makes this furniture easily to recognize. The major styles resemble oversized pieces from the Empire Period. This furniture is very durable, although it was cheaply made.

72   From Darkness To Light

Art Nouveau: **A)** *Tiffany wisteria lamp* **B)** *Table with flowing lines* **C)** *Favrile glass candleholder*

Art Nouveau sterling silver brush

Art Nouveau brass mirror

Arts and Crafts & Mission (1905-1920)

This style was extremely linear and almost void of decoration. The famous craftsmen during this period were Elbert Hubbard, Gustav Stickley and Frank Lloyd Wright. Finer pieces during this period include Tiger (Quarter-sawn) oak pieces. The hardware used was hammered copper. Good pieces will have dovetailing in the back and front. Upholstered mission pieces with original green, red or brown leather are highly sought after. Oak was the main wood used.

ARTS AND CRAFTS & MISSION: A) *Sofa* B) *Library table*

Art Deco (1920-1950)

Manufacturers of this type of furniture replaced the flowing lines of Art Nouveau with straight lines and space-age designs. Plastic and chrome were used with furniture. Naugahyde (simulated leather,) was used to cover plastic chairs, sofas. and other furnishings. Other items include art pottery, ironstone, floor model radios, porcelain, Bakelite (a type of plastic) and jewelry. Bleached and burled woods were used to create sleek furniture designs. Art Deco is still available today.

An Eccentric Thought: Blending Antiques with African Motifs & Furnishings!

Knowing the periods and styles of furniture will make you an educated buyer as you veer into the world of auctions and estate sales. As you peruse magazines, watch television, visit favorite stores and decorate your home—try to match feet, legs, and aprons with periods, styles, and designs. It's thrilling to be able to identify a Chippendale chair or a Hepplewhite sideboard. But, have you considered blending antiques with African motifs and furnishings? Try it! You will discover something new and exciting!

As African-Americans in the 90's, our style has become more reflective of how we actually live. A growing number of people are infusing their lives with rich African flavor, from kente cloth to adinkra symbols. Over the last few decades, a rich explosion of interest in African styles has been birthed in "Africa's New World Children." A rapid growth in resources to fuel this interest is evident in many urban centers. There are new galleries and shops specializing in African motifs on everything from greeting cards, office furnishings and tablewear to drapes, kitchen items and children's apparel.

As African-Americans recapture historical riches, we will have to revisit the rich textiles, colorful accessories, and sculptural designs of Africa. Imagine the creative and aesthetic beauty of African designs coupled with cherished heirlooms or antique pieces! Like cabinetmaker, Thomas Day or story Quilter, Harriet Powers, we can bring our ancestral culture to impact and define our modern world, work and living space!

Our homes should display our finest possessions, and "showcase treasures of the past, favorite family momentos and wonderful finds from near and far." We can decorate from our life experiences and blend cultural heritage with fine antiques, add a wealth of meaning, history and beauty to our lives.

Interior designers, Sharne Algotsson and Denys Davis have written an excellent book on how "Africa's colors, patterns, textiles, art, furniture, and traditions can enrich any home." The book is entitled, *The Spirit of African Designs* (Clarkson N. Potter, New York, 1996), and it is filled with colorful photos and stunning illustrations that will stimulate your creative ideas. You will gain practical insight on how to collect, use, and decorate with African designs. Look for this book at your favorite bookstore.

With your new knowledge of antiques and eclectic ideas for decorating your home, you are ready for a good, shopping spree! Happy Antiquing!

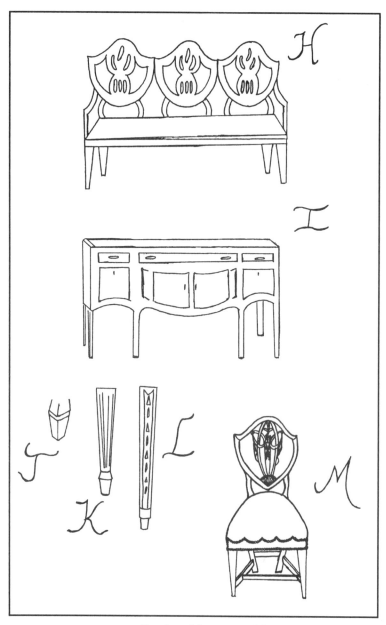

Continued from page 66
H) *Settee*   **I)** *Sideboard*   **J)** *Spade foot*   **K)** *Tapered foot with reeding*
L) *Tapered foot*   **M)** *Shield back chair with brass tacks.*

col-lec'tion - 1. Act or process of collecting. 2. That which is collected; an assemblage; an accumulation.

Webster's Collegiate Dictionary

CHAPTER 6

ADMIRING & APPRECIATING COLLECTIBLES
An Inventory of Household Valuables

A collectible could be anything from buttons to baseball cards. Most collectibles are displayed at home in some form or fashion. Larger items such as furniture, automobiles and boats may not be suitable to display in large quantities. A collectible can be an antique, semi-antique or something brand new. It simply takes someone to assemble and accumulate similar items and instantly we have a collectible!

In this section, we will feature common collectibles that may be found around your house. You know, all of that "stuff" we have crammed into our cupboards, closets, attics and basements over the years. Common collectibles have been categorized to help in your search. Categories include glassware, porcelain trans lucente, semi-porcelain, pottery, linen and jewelry.

However, if your home is much too modern to contain these "older treasures," then take a good look at Grandmother's things or those of older relatives. You'll be surprise to find that ordinary pieces from the past, have an increasing popularity among collectors today!

Glassware
The most common collectible found around the American home is Depression glass. This glassware was made primarily during the Depression era, between 1920 and

the late 1930's. The colors made were amber, blue, black, green, pink, red, yellow and white. This inexpensive glass has had a recent surge in popularity. Condition is very important, however. Chips, cracks and scratches will significantly deflect the value.

Depression glassware includes dinner sets, ovenware,

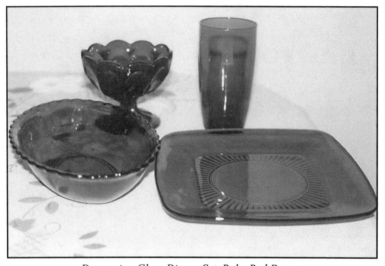

Depression Glass Dinner Set, Ruby Red Pattern

canister sets, dessert sets, vases and candlesticks. This glassware is available in different patterns and some are more sought after than others.

But, all glassware is not the same! Other valuable glass found around many households may include:

Milk Glass - An opaque glass that is white and resembles milk. It comes in various colors, such as, blue, green pink and black.

Cut Glass - Patterns are cut into the glass, showing a clear, crystal prism of colors. The edges are cut sharp and angular. There are many different patterns. Examples of fine, heavy cut glass would include punch bowls, decanters, pitchers, candy dishes, vases and lamps.

Pressed Glass – A lightweight glass made by pressing patterns into a mold. The edges are round and irregular.

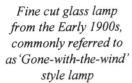

Fine cut glass lamp from the Early 1900s, commonly referred to as 'Gone-with-the-wind' style lamp

This is an inexpensive glass normally used for everyday dining. Examples of pressed glass include goblets, cakestands, and covered compotes.

Art Glass - This glass is considered an art form because it was designed using different artistic methods and patterns. Art glass has a varying array of design styles, manufacturers and techniques. Common names would include Handel, Tiffany, Carnival and Bohemian.

Handel: Handel was a maker of fine art glass. He is famous for his glass shade lamps and vases. These pieces are highly sought after and extremely valuable. They sell

Pressed glass punch bowl

Signed early 1900s Handel lamp (art glass shade)

for hundreds and thousands of dollars.

Tiffany Glass: Lewis Comfort Tiffany was also famous for his art glass designs. His handmade iridescent glass was called *favrile*. Most of his lamp shapes have floral or geometric designs. Tiffany stained glass windows, vases and lampshades are very expensive and highly sought. His father, Charles L. Tiffany was founder of Tiffany and Company of New York City. His jewelry products were made of the finest quality and his name is a symbol of excellence, even today.

Carnival Glass: These glass pieces like tumblers, pitchers, vases, bowls and candy dishes that were frequently given away at carnivals, from 1905 to the 1920s. It is an iridescent glass that includes common colors like marigold, green, aqua, blue, purple, and peach.

Bohemian Glass: This Victorian glass has a color overlay that has been etched or cut to clear crystal to form a design. The most common color is ruby.

Miscellaneous: Other glass designers include Heisey, Fenton, Fostoria, Pairpoint, Steuben, Imperial and Anchor Hocking, Galle', and Cambridge. These glass pieces will have signature markings on the bottom, to indicate the designer.

Carnival glass tumbler. Highly collectible since the 1950s.

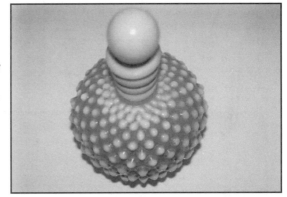

Depression glass perfume bottle, Hobnail pattern.

Porcelain Trans Lucente

Porcelain Trans Lucente is simply porcelain that you can see through. Porcelain refers to more than expensive dinnerware (or china). It may include vases, figurines, lamps, bowls, candleholders and much more.

Over time, some porcelain will develop little mosaic cracks called "crazing." This may indicate an *aged* piece. A way to determine the date of porcelain is by looking at its bottom. If the piece has the name of a country on it such as England, Japan, China, or France, then the piece was made after 1891. If the word "made in" appears in addition to the country of origin, then the porcelain was made after 1914. Do not assume that the piece is valuable if there are no markings. Most valuable items are generally signed. Popular porcelain manufacturers of trans lucente include Haviland, Limoges, Sevres, Capo-di-monte, Lladro and Meissen.

Lladro porcelain figurine of young black girl

Semi-Porcelain

Semi-porcelain is opaque (dull, without luster) and

you can not see through it. This type of porcelain is commonly known as Ironstone. It is durable earthenware that comes in a variety of forms. Semi-porcelain designs by Homer Laughlin, Fiesta, Wedgwood, Spode, Willow, Johnson Brothers, Blue Flow, Occupied Japan and Staffordshire are highly collectible.

Occupied Japan cup and saucer. These pieces were made after World War II, when United States occupied Japan.

Pottery

Pottery refers to both the hard, non-porous stoneware and the softer porous earthenware. It is even more opaque in comparison to porcelain and also heavier. The condition of pottery is very important. Chips and cracks will decrease the value of a piece. Common pottery that may be found in most household include Hull, Roseville, Shawnee, Weller, Rookwood, Van Briggle, Blue Ridge, Watts, Bennington and McCoy.

Linens

Most of the linens common to modern households were made during the Victorian era through the 1950's. These linens were used to decorate beds, chairs, tables and other household furnishings. Older linens that were once packed in trunks, have had a recent surge in popularity.

Many of the decorator magazines include time-less items used in combination with modern pieces of furni-

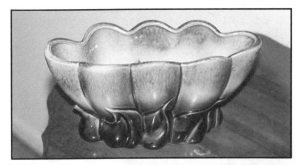

Art pottery bowl from the 1940s-1950s, unsigned

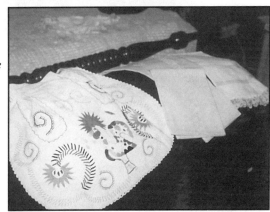

Embroidered apron, hand-made pillowcases and crocheted guest towel
Photograph by Leon Stoudemire

ture. It is very common to see crocheted bedspreads, embroidered pillowcases and cotton sheets used in combination with newer pieces. Doilies, quilts, coverlets, tablecloths and runners seem to fit quite well with new decor. Here are a few helpful techniques to address the issues of stains, storage and general cleaning with older linens:

Stain Removal: Stains can be removed from most white pieces by mixing 1 tsp. sodium perborate with 1 gallon of water, then soaking for several hours. This solution will remove most stains and produce beautiful linen for you to display.

Storage: When storing large spreads and quilts, try to roll and not fold them. Folding develops creases, weakens the fibers and causes tears in the fabric. Proper storing is extremely important to preserving your linens.

General Cleaning: The use of starches and other chemicals over a period of time will also weaken fabrics. Do not use harsh detergents such as, Clorox. Ivory Snow and Wiz will gently clean your linens without harming them.

Jewelry

Jewelry has always been favorably regarded. Used to adorn, these items have special meaning. Jewelry is valued based on the metals used, quality of stones, and artistic merit. Jewelry with precious stones, such as diamonds and pearls, require an expert jewelry appraisal.

Collectible crystal glass beads

Presently, costume jewelry has grown in popularity. Bakelite, which is a collectible plastic jewelry made from the early 1900's through the 1940's, is highly sought after. Necklaces and bracelets made with glass and crystal beads are very popular. As jewelry businesses closed, their pieces increased in value. Signed pieces from the jewelry lines of Coro, Miriam Haskell, Sarah Coventry, Eisenberg, Lisner, Trifari, Weiss and Danescraft are highly collectible. Rhinestones, crystals, black glass

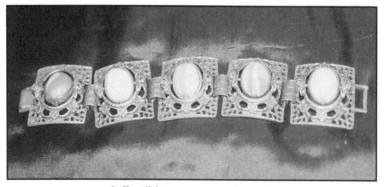

Collectible moon stone bracelet

beads, and jewelry pieces made of silver and gold are always valuable.

Mixing Antiques & Collectibles with
Modern Decor - The number of antique, collectible,
decorating and lifestyle magazines have increased significantly. These magazines cater to different interests and styles from the sleek and upscale to the country and homespun. Despite their varying audiences, these magazines have helped to increase the country's appreciation for historical treasures. Articles visually enhance our awareness by combining different styles, fabrics, and accessories with antiques and collectibles to create stunning looks. For example, an early 1900's table could be used in one room as a desk. Or a collection of old baskets could line a staircase or windowsill. An eclectic school of decorating is sweeping the country and saying, "Anything goes! Pick your style! Mix and match!"

Heavily carved room divider
Photograph by Leon Stoudemire

It is not always necessary for antiques and collectibles to be in excellent condition. Less than perfect items often function well in new roles. A piece of cracked pottery which once held fresh flowers could be used to display silk ones.

While not everyone likes the use of antiques in every décor, there are certainly renewed uses for older pieces. It is not always necessary to alter old furniture, but upholstery is a good way to accentuate a new room. Placing an old chair or table in a modern room could add a special 'touch of class' or a splash of elegance.

Mixing antiques and collectibles with modern designs

is really exciting! Old pieces of crochet maybe sewn onto new pillows to create a connection to the past. Pie safes can be used in the kitchen to display dishes. Washstands work well as small cabinets in bathrooms to store toiletries. Let your mind be creative and find new uses for old pieces.

American Art pottery

"We have sat on the river bank and caught catfish with pin hooks. [Now] the time has come to harpoon a whale."
JOHN HOPE, C. 1900

CHAPTER 7

SAVING AGELESS ITEMS & COLLECTING FADELESS FINDS
What To Save from the past and Collect for the future

In this chapter we will answer the two questions heard most often, "What kinds of things do I keep?" and "What sort of items should I look for at sales?" First, you will be able to review a brief listing of various items that are considered " valuable collectibles." Many of these things you will already have around your home. They should not be casually tossed, but preserved for years to come.

As we enter the 21st Century, a great number of our common, household memorabilia will drastically increase in value. You will want to be among those who planned for the future and kept your *ageless items* in tack!

In the latter part of the chapter, we outline collectible items you should collect while out shopping in non-traditional shopping arenas. These are your *fadeless finds* that almost never loose their value. Shopping for collectibles is a great adventure. So, have a lot of fun!

"Don't Throw It Away!" - Items To *Save* In Changing Times

The following is a list of items you will want to save as we enter the year 2000. Every aspect of life and work in the 20th century will be collectible – so don't throw *everything* away! Take the time to organize your attic, basement or closets as you look for these valuable items.

Newspapers
It is an excellent idea to save newspapers with major historic headlines. The more international the event, the more valuable it will be. When saving newspapers, lay them flat in a book or place in a plastic wrapper. Folded newspaper will turn brown or even tear at the folds.

Magazines
Magazines with an extraordinary cover feature, typographical error or a special edition would be important to keep. Copies of older magazines to collect would include *Life, Ebony, Look, Sepia, Jet, Harper's Weekly* and *National Geographic*. A few current magazines to keep your eye on would include *Essence, Time, Emerge, Newsweek* and *Black Enterprise*.

Life magazine depicting the funeral procession of the late JFK, circa 1963.

Books
Books are very collectible! Look for first editions, autographed books, recalled books, leather bound books, art books, children's books, cookbooks, garden books and almanacs. Books written by or about celebrities increase in value very quickly. Books based on

Antique leather bound books, circa 1838 to 1896.

movies like *Gone with the Wind, Forrest Gump,* and *Bridges of Madison County* are good to keep because they will increase in value. Classic literature written by well-known and established writers such as William Shakespeare, Mark Twain or John Steinbeck are also important to hold on to. More recent classic works of literature by Richard Wright, Zora Neale Hurston, Toni Morrison or Maya Angelou will grow more into collectibles with the turn of the century. History books common to a particular region or state are highly collectible. Present-day books based on television heroes like *Tarzan, Lord of the Jungle, Superman, and Batman,* as well as, modern children's books featuring *Barney, Dr. Seus,* and *Sesame Street* should be preserved. Never miss a library book sale! They are a great place to purchase many of these kinds of books.

Kitchenware
Most old kitchen utensils, bowls and furnishings will have great value. Wooden or metal iceboxes, hand-operated washing machines, old washboards, irons, toasters, blenders and other appliances from the kitchen of yesteryear all appeal to collectors.

Sewing Items
Items common to an old sewing box like thimbles, buttons, knitting needles, pincushions, and sewing birds are high on the collectible list. Also look for important pieces of lace or other valuable fabric accessories. Of course older dated sewing machines are always sought.

Office Furnishings
There is always a good market for old sturdy desks, chairs and file cabinets. Also, lawyer's bookcases and glass-fronted units made of wood can bring a lot of money. Old typewriters, adding machines and telephones are considered archaic and have

Antique L.C. Smith typewriter
Photo by: Leon Stoudemire

have depreciated in value. But, collectors do exist even for these items.

Toys

Old toys have always fascinated people. Adults who maintain toy collections are able to relish former times of play when little responsibility was required of them. Collectible toys would include the Rebuke's Cube, jigsaw puzzles, clowns, McDonalds items, mechanical banks, old metal cars and trucks, metal games (like Chinese Checkers and Monopoly) Lionel trains, metal boats and tractors, Schwinn bikes, sleighs, G.I. Joe, Fat Albert & the Gang, Popeye and other cartoon characters.

Dolls

Below you will find a list of popular dolls that should be saved. Many are highly collectible and others will be in the next century.

Brooke Shields	Shirley Temple	Annie
Bozo	Rambo	Cabbage Patch
Gizmo	Tickle Me Elmo	Star Trek
Beanie Babies	Star Wars	Tuskegee Airmen
Ms. Pac Man	Michael Jackson	Fat Albert
Barbie	G.I. Joe (*General*)	Betty Boo
Hulk Hogan	Howdie Doodie	Madame Alexander
Geraldine (*Flip Wilson*)	Julia (*Diahann Carroll*)	

Political Memorabilia

Political items increase in popularity with time. Political memorabilia would include: campaign buttons, flags, speeches, records, newspapers, photographs, autographed documents, posters, promotional slogans, commemorative plates, and other memorabilia. A few historical and current politicians to collect are:

Jimmy Carter	John F. Kennedy	Abraham Lincoln
Richard Nixon	Nelson Mandela	Martin Luther King
George Washington	Teddy Roosevelt	Ronald Reagan
Bill Clinton	Thomas Jefferson	Jessie Jackson

Media & Entertainment Memorabilia

Memorabilia from popular television shows and sitcoms have increased in popularity in recent years. Collectible items would include tee shirts, caps, posters, autographed pictures, and other promotional items. A listing of a few popular TV shows from the 60's, 70's and 80's are:

Mash	Dynasty	Brady Bunch
Lone Ranger	Leave It to Beaver	Big Valley & Bonanza
Happy Days	Andy Griffith	Dark Shadows
Lost In Space	Gilligan's Island	Julia
Spiderman	Batman	Dallas

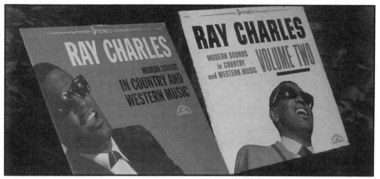

Early Ray Charles albums are highly sought by collectors.

Music

You will want to keep phonograph records; concert programs; records in their original jackets; sheet music; promotional posters, and other items from famous singers and musicians like:

Jimi Hendrix	Michael Jackson	Elvis Pressley
The Beatles	John Lennon	Garth Brooks
Mahalia Jackson	Duke Ellington	Nat King Cole
All Motown Artists	Roy Orbison	Ray Charles

Sports

Sports memorabilia is highly collectible. Important items to keep include ticket stubs, souvenir programs, promotional posters, baseball cards, original athletic clothing, signed balls or gloves; photographs of players, and other athletic gear or advertising items. A few famous athletes to collect are:

Muhammad Ali	Joe Louis	Jackie Robinson
Satchel Paige	Tiger Woods	Negro Baseball League
Pete Rose	Arnold Palmer	Bear Bryant
Mickey Mantel	Babe Ruth	Michael Jordan
Hank Aaron	Willie Mays	Harlem Globetrotters

Miscellaneous

Other items you will want to save and collect would be movie posters, advertising labels, stamped postcards, historic documents, picture frames, legal documents, comic books, vintage clothing and jewelry, fishing memorabilia, fire and police items, and World Fair collectibles.

Remember, if these valuable collectibles are not 'tucked away' at your new home, they may definitely be at Grandma's place or another older relative. So, take the time to search around, now that you know what to look for!

"Yes! Take That Home!" - Important Items To Collect In Changing Times

Many of us cannot boast of having "old things" around the house. Perhaps you were born in the last 30 years and have filled your home with modern things. Well do not fret, here is a listing of important items you can "collect" while shopping at auction, attending an estate sales or cruising the thrift stores and flea markets.

Antique towel rack showcase embroidered & appliquéd hand towels of varying colors and fabrics. Photo: Leon Stoudemire

Linens and Textiles

Crocheted bedspreads, tablecloths, doilies and coverlets are a must have. Handwork can command high prices in antique shops. These lovely pieces have grown significantly in popularity and are enjoying new uses. Pieces of crochet can be used as pillow covers, furniture protectors, and window treatments. Chenille spreads will add lovely appeal to any bed. However, condition is essential!

Embroidery
Embroidered pillowcases, sheets, tablecloths, spreads, doilies, or any type of hand-done needlework has had a recent surge in popularity. Many grandmothers and great-grand mothers created these beautiful pieces of handwork. These decorative items have found renewed use as pillow covers, bed coverings, and tablecloths, particularly if they are in good condition. Fragile pieces can be placed in shadowbox frames to make interesting wall coverings.

Quilts
Once used strictly for warmth, quilts have now emerged as works of art. Quilts vary in design and color. The ones that are entirely hand-made command the greatest prices. Popular patterns include the wedding ring, morning star, log cabin and patchwork patterns.

When looking at quilts look for flowing patterns and intricate design. When trying to determine the skills of quilters, take out a ruler and count the number of stitches per inch in a section of quilt. Once you have a count, multiply by two. Twenty stitches or more to the inch are considered crafts of superior skill.

Women often went blind making these quilts. Our foremothers invested much pride and time into this historical art form. They worked diligently with their hands, in an attempt to pass on an article that would provide personal warmth and a family treasure for many generations. Quilts are an excellent investment!

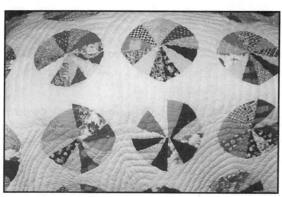

Pieced quilt, circa early 1900's, Grove Hill, Alabama
Photo: Leon Stoudemire

Old Photography

Old photographed postcards reflect the faces and styles of the past.

Old photographs, especially those in their old frames are highly sought. As always, old photographs of famous people command higher prices. These collectibles are viewed for their artistic merit and contribution to history.

Architectural Antiques

This can be anything from crystal doorknobs to stain glass windows. Crystal door knobs once graced older houses and may command as much as $30 dollars per knob to a collector, or someone refurbishing an old house. Other items include doors, mantels, hardwood floors, columns, locks, ceramic tiles, and brasses.

Numerous architectural specialty shops are opening across the country to meet a growing demand for antique hardware in the restoration of older homes.

American Art Pottery

American Art pottery was fashioned as bowls, jugs, wall pockets, cookie jars, pitcher/bowl sets and vases. Most American pottery, regardless of age, can bring nice prices. It is not unheard of for collectors to pay thousands for rare and highly collectible pieces. Common names of pottery found around many households include Bennington, Blue Ridge, Hull, McCoy, Red Wing, Rookwood, Roseville, Shawnee, Van Briggle, Watts, and Weller.

Coin silver and sterling silver flatware are very collectible. These coin silver pieces were buried during the Civil War by a Southern family and purchased at an estate sale.
Photo: Leon Stoudemire

Sterling Silver

Sterling silver is by far more expensive than silver plate. However, some old silver plate, depending on a maker such as Sheffield, can be very valuable. Sterling pieces including flatware, tea sets, bowls, candle holders, brushes, and powder jars will be marked 925, silver, sterling or STG. If these marks are not present, there may be a symbol to denote the company name and silver content. Purchase a price guide to begin recognizing some of the common names, symbols, and prices of silver. The more common names in plate and sterling are Gorham, Oneida, Reed and Barton, Sheffield, Towle, and Wallace. Old pewter (which resembles a dull silver color) is also very collectible, especially the early American pieces.

Star Wars

All of the toys, dolls, posters and other memorabilia from the *Star Wars* trilogy are very collectible. Recently an item bought for $2.00 sold for $250.00. Be on the look out for *Star Trek* also, which can command high prices also.

Dolls

Popular dolls like Shirley Temple and Barbie, particularly, from the 50's may sell for up to $8,000.00. The G.I. Joe doll is very collectible. A recent auction in 1993, showed the highest amount ever paid for a doll was $231,000,000 for a 1884 Black French doll made for the worlds fair. Other collectible dolls include Madame Alexander, French Jumeau, and Cabbage Patch to name a few.

Newspapers and Magazines

Newspapers reporting historical events are very collectible. For example, the bombing of Pearl Harbor, or the assassination of famous people like, John F. Kennedy, Martin Luther King or John Lennon are worth keeping. Papers and magazines featuring the late Diana, Princess of Wales have increased in value since her untimely death. There are collectors who specialize in selling these papers for hefty prices.

The magazine, *T.V. Guide* is very collectible, especially those featuring The Beetles, Elvis, Star Wars, or famous people from the 60's and 70's. Other magazines to collect would include *Life, Ebony, Look, Jet, Harper's Weekly* and *National Geographic*, and *Harper's Weekly* to name a few.

Toys

There is a growing collectors market for antique and semi-antique toys. Games from the 50's to 60's command good prices. Examples would include old Monopoly, Scrabble games, Chinese Checkers, Chess sets, and other dated games. Metal cars and trucks are also in demand.

Holiday Items

Old Valentine cards, Halloween decorations, Thanksgiving items, and Christmas ornaments are very collectible. Even postcards and greeting cards from these holidays are good to hold on to. The older the better. These items may be worth up to several hundred dollars.

Disney Collectibles

The famous Mickey Mouse is highly collectible. Most collectors seek just about anything from the World of Disney including clocks, watches, dolls, and other promotional materials. Other characters are collectible, but they may not yield as much as Mickey. Disneyana made in the 1930's will bring the highest prices.

Smoking Items

These collectibles include cigar molds, cutters, labels, tobacco figures, cigar boxes and tobacco tins. While you are cruising the sales, be on the lookout for these items.

Fishing Memorabilia

Fishing rods, lures and reels made from the early 1800's on are highly collectible. Reels and lures in excellent condition are the most desirable.

Pocket knives on display for a recent estate sale.

Legal Documents, Letters and Diaries

Dated letters describing special events or important topics of the day are important to collect. Of course, when the author or receiver of such letters is famous, the price will increase dramatically. Cancelled stamps on these letters (when present) may also be valuable.

Old diaries describing circumstances during an historic period are highly collectible. Legal documents, relating to a specific period or event may be of value as well.

Diploma from Madam C.J. Waker School of Beauty. Madam Walker was the first African-American millionaire in the U.S.

Miscellaneous

Other items you will want to collect would be old bottles, picture frames, fountain pens, music boxes, jewelry, cast iron banks, Civil War items, slave documents, pocket knives and other cutlery.

German music box and photo album, still plays beautiful musical tunes.

> "I am of the African race, and in the colour ... of the deepest dye, and it is under a sense of the most profound gratitude to the Supreme Ruler."
>
> BENJAMIN BANNEKER

CHAPTER 8

COLOR ME BLACK!
Putting A Spotlight on Black Collectibles

Black items have been collected in America since the 18th century. From the very beginning, these items showcased derogatory images of black people in various modes of life and work.

Handmade collectibles were made prior to the 1900's and include folk items, wooden dolls, paintings of slaves, black rag dolls, single portraits, paintings of farm workers, and furnishings. When found, these items are very expensive.

From 1900 to the 1950's, advertisers and manufacturers used images of blacks on their sales products. Many of these items were considered amusing in nature and were used as souvenirs. Decorated spoons, dolls, prints, photographs, movie posters, sheet music, food labels and other promotional items were mass produced using black caricatures.

Between 1950 and the 1970's, images of blacks changed from "degrading caricatures to more realistic images." Black collectibles during this period include dolls, slave documents, mammy cookie jars, salt and pepper shakers, spoon rest, shopping peg boards, and condiment sets to name a few. Both white and black artisans made these items.

Black collectibles were not only produced in America. They were also manufactured in Japan, Germany, France,

England, China, Africa and Australia. These items provide a close-up view of how the entire world viewed the African-American.

Today, there is a "wide range of collectible Black items which reflect both the changing times of our country and the change of attitude towards Black people."

Famous, civil-rights activist, Julian Bond has amassed a huge collection of black memorabilia. In the following paragraph, Bond describes the world of "black collectibles" from an African-American perspective that we all can understand:

> "For others, like myself, these artifacts also summon up yesterday's world, but in our hands and homes they become reminders of a different sort. They speak of triumph and overcoming, and inform us that despite what others thought and believed, we were never what these figurines and objects suggest. We see them as sentinels guarding the past, doorkeepers who prevent our ever returning to it, harsh—if even sometimes beautiful—preservers of the history we have overthrown. Their presence on my shelves steels me against that past. Despite their generally small size, they shout at me as I pass by—'Look at me! I am not what I seem[10].'"

Like Julian Bond, we should learn from these past images and push forward to greater heights of greatness. African-American collectors of black memorabilia are helping us to do exactly that. Malinda Saunders, and Jeanette Carson were instrumental in founding the 1st Annual Black Memorabilia Show and Sale in October of 1984. This unique event was held in Silver Springs, Maryland and brought together black and white collectors from around the country.

The late Steven Lewis, collector and curator of the Lewis-Blalock Collection describes this important show and the personal effect it had on his life. "I eagerly witnessed firsthand the unveiling of precious artifacts as they were unwrapped and placed into position for public viewing and purchase," writes Lewis. "Often I felt in awe of and amazed by these rare icons of history, each with its own history, each with its own story about the pride and pain of a people--*my* people[11]."

In a sense, black memorabilia had found its way home, back to the African-American community. Black collectors are on the increase, recapturing our history and collecting the pieces of our broken past. Without doubt, there is a new appreciation for these historic artifacts.

Collecting black memorabilia will stimulate your senses and arouse your emotions. But *remembering* is part of our journey. In the wisdom of SANKOFA, we must "return and fetch that which was lost, and move forward with it."

Below we have outlined a brief listing of Black collectibles you will want to save and collect:

Historical Items
Any memorabilia of African-American cowboys or the Buffalo soldiers are valuable historical artifacts. You will want to preserve slave documents, Bibles with recorded births and deaths, Jim Crow signs, and photographs.

Jim Crow signs from the 1930s reveal the segregation of Selma, Alabama, public pools and other racial feelings of the times, value $50.

Kitchen Items
Valuable kitchen collectibles would include condiment sets, salt & pepper shakers, black mammy cookie jars, wall clocks and decorations, shopping peg boards, toothpick holders, water pitchers and cookbooks.

Rockingham mammy cookie jar, value $400 - $600

F & F salt & pepper shaker, value $45-$75

Toys & Games

Toys are highly valuable in the world of collectibles. Look for mechanical toys, pull trucks, windup tins toys, African figures, tin noisemakers, plastic clowns, board games (like "The Cake Walk," or "The Coon Hunt"), and card games (like "Old Maid").

Commercial Advertising

There are a host of collectibles featuring blacks in advertising. Items to collect would include: candy wrappers, cereal labels, boxed cleansers, church or funeral home fans, match boxes, perfume labels, and trade cards.

Look specifically for Coon Chicken Inn items, advertising tins (featuring Luzianne coffee, Aunt Jemima pancake mix and Cream of Wheat products), and 'yellowing' newspaper and magazine ads.

Bull Durham smoking tobacco advertisement, value $150-$250

Black Figurals

Black figurals of clocks, doorstops, ceramic figurines, bottles, mugs, pincushions, water pitchers, lawn figurines, statutes and vases are highly collectible.

Diaper Dan thermometer, value $45 - $65

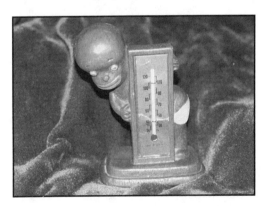

Music & Records

You will want to keep phonograph records, concert programs, L&P Records with original jackets, sheet music, R&B posters of Motown singing groups like the Supremes & Temptations, albums of famous musicians like Mahalia Jackson, Otis Redding, Charlie Parker, Jimi Hendrix, B.B. King, James Brown and others.

Amos 'n Andy - 3 record set circa 1979, value $15 - $30.

Paper Collectibles

Do not throw away autographed photos or books of famous African-Americans, children's books like *Little Black Sambo* & *Little Brown Koko*, decals, posters, historic letters written by and about black people, and historic issues of *Ebony* or *Jet* magazine.

*Special Issue of **Ebony** featuring Frederick Douglas, 'Founder of the Protest Movement' in commemoration of the 100th Anniversary of "The Emancipation Proclamation," September, 1963. Value $15 - $30.*

Political Memorabilia

Be sure to preserve political memorabilia from the 50's & 60's (featuring groups like the Black Panthers, NAACP, and the Southern Christian Leadership Conference or featuring important leaders like Malcolm X, Martin Luther King, and John F. Kennedy), pinback buttons with photo promotions or political slogans; badges representing political campaigns; historic booklets, posters or fliers of political events; photographs, record albums; commemorative ribbons; certificates with signatures, and handwritten notes or letters would make a fine collection.

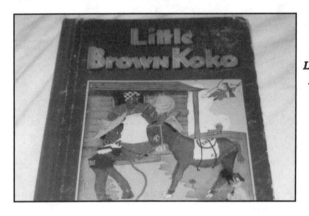

Little Brown KoKo, circa 1951
value
$35 - $50

Dolls
Black cloth dolls, Black Barbies, paper cut-outs, paper dolls and puppets are excellent collectibles.

Sports Memorabilia
Sports memorabilia is highly collectible. Collect historic baseball tickets, advertising posters, promotional pieces, baseball cards, clothing items like caps or jerseys, signatures of athletes, and photographs of players.

Miscellaneous
Ashtrays and ashtray stands, carved pipes, cigar boxes, humidors (which held loose tobacco), label folk art; mechanical, tin and still banks; and stamps featuring famous African-Americans like George Washington Carver, Frederick Douglas and Benjamin Banneker.

Darkie Toothpaste 1940-1950s
value,
$35 - $45

The new Black collectibles including figurines of such famous persons as Rosa Parks & Sojourner Truth to common folk like a church-going lady and watermelon boy.

There is a new interest in internationally known dancer, Josephine Baker and Hollywood actress, Dorothy Dandridge. Any memorabilia of these famous stars will be valuable collectibles. Modern figurines or pieces from the 'new Black collectibles' such as, the "All God's Children" series will also be important to hold on to.

As you begin your collection, beware of the reproductions, coming from foreign countries, that are being cheaply made and marketed today. "The important thing to remember when collecting is to buy the very best for your money," writes P.J. Gibbs, author of *Black Collectibles: Sold In America*. "If you decide to collect only decorative Black spoons, buy the best. Do not be tempted by the low cost of inferior quality items. You may have only a few items at the end of a year's search but your collectibles will be of a higher quality."

---

[10] Kyle Husfloen, ed. *Black Americana Price Guide: A Comprehensive, Illustrated Guide to African-American Collectibles of the 19th & 20th Centuries*. Dubuque, IA: Antique Trader Books, 1996, p. vii.

[11] Reno, Dawn E. *The Encyclopedia of Black Collectibles: A Value and Identification Guide*. Radnor, PA: Wallace-Homestead Books, 1996, p. x.

PART IV

Welcome To The Exciting World of Auctions

No more auction block for me,
No more, no more,
No more auction block for me,
Many thousands gone.
A NEGRO SPIRITUAL

CHAPTER 9

FROM AUCTION BLOCK TO AUCTION GAVEL!
Reclaiming Pride, Regaining Power

Auctions began thousands of years ago. The Greek historian, Heredotus wrote about auctions. Babylonian maidens were auctioned off in marriage to the highest bidder. But it was the Romans who were the first to formally license auctioneers. In Latin, the word auction is referred to as *auction shub hasta*, which means, "under the spear." Romans used the spear to signal the beginning of an auction event.

The Pilgrims brought this exciting marketing technique to the Americas. They were instrumental in transferring the English method of auction into their new lives in the colonies.

Our first president, George Washington was a frequent auction buyer. He furnished his home at Mt. Vernon, as well as other residences, with rare treasures from auction sales.

Even military spoils from the Civil War were auctioned off to the highest bidder. The union army used persons of colonel designation to conduct official auctions. To this day, the title of Colonel is given to all auctioneers.

Overcoming The Auction Block

Auctions also included the selling of African people as slaves to Southern landowners. The auction block painfully represents the most degrading form of human injustice in the history of the New World. African-Americans can vividly recall the viciousness with which our ancestors were bought and sold into slavery. As descendants of slaves, the memory of such realities conjures up angry feelings. Historian, John Hope Franklin in *From Slavery to Freedom,* writes about the casual and business attitude that permeated the auctioning of slaves:

> "many business firms that dealt in farm supplies and animals frequently carried a 'line' of slaves. Auctioneers who disposed of real estate and personal property sold slaves along with their other commodities. Planters...advertised in the newspapers that they had slaves for sale. Foreign visitors to the nation's capitol were puzzled at the sight of slave auction blocks, slave jails and slave pens."

A system that once stripped us of our human dignity can now empower us with economic stability; and provide a direct means of recapturing "riches" that can be passed on to the next generation. Time has a way of turning all things around. As descendants of slaves, we can now wield the auction gavel with wisdom and power. Becoming active participants in auctions or choosing auctioning as a profession can be the healing and restoration we need in this historic arena. We can bring new light to the dark 'auction block' of our past. New and exciting adventures are before us.

Auctioning as a Profession

Would you like to meet interesting people? Sell wonderful things? Start a new part-time or full-time career? And earn an endless income? If the answer is "Yes!" to these questions, then the auction profession may be for you. An exciting world of opportunities is open to auctioneers! You will have a chance to serve a varying client base, learn a host of interesting facts and increase your overall assets.

On any given day, there is no telling what kind of merchandise you will be asked to sell. Although some auctioneers do specialize. These areas of specialty can include real estate, cattle & livestock, exotic animals, automobiles and personal property. Others, however, choose to sell real estate or do fundraising auctions exclusively.

In addition to specializing, auctioneers can do relief (or fill-in) work for various auction companies or they may choose to set up their own auction house. Basic business rules and normal regulations apply.

The start-up cost for this profession is nominal, starting as low as, $1,000 for business cards, licenses, brochures and minor equipment. A very successful business can be run out of your home, so no formal office setting is required. As with any other profession - hard work, dedication and tenacity finishes the race.

Auctioning is probably better respected today than it has ever been. This area of marketing is growing by leaps and bounds. And, again, it is wide open to African-American professionals.

Auctioneers work on commission and are generally paid a percentage of what they sale. For example, if you sell a $100,000 estate and negotiate a commission of 20%, then you will receive $20,000 for that sale. Of course advertising and labor costs have to be deducted. There are not many jobs where you can make $20,000 in one day!

While sitting in an auction class, I can remember a world champion auctioneer saying, "Most people are not rich today, because they are too busy going to work." There's a lot of hidden wisdom in this statement.

Provided below is a listing of licensing agencies for every state in the country. Most states require an auctioneer license to practice. This is due in part to past abuse by 'fly-by-night' shysters fronting as auctioneers. Check directly with your state agency for information on their rules and regulations. Even when a state does not require a state license, auctions may still be governed by a local municipality or county commission. Also contact the:

National Auctioneers Association
880 Ballentine, Overland Park, Kansas 66214.
(913) 541-8084, fax (913) 894-5281
email at naah@aol.com for membership, training and conference information.

State Auctioneer Licensing Agencies

ALABAMA
State Board of Auctioneers
Post Office Box 56
Montgomery, AL 36101
(334) 263-3407

ALASKA
Division of Occupational Licensing
3601 C Street
Suite #722
Anchorage, AK 99503
(907) 563-2169

ARIZONA
Department of Revenue
License and Registration Section
1600 W. Monroe
Phoenix, AR 85007
(602) 542-2076, ext.50

CALIFORNIA
The California Auctioneer Commission has been discontinued. No license required.

COLORADO
Division of Real Estate
1776 Logan Street
Denver, CO 80203
(303) 894-2166

CONNECTICUT
Connecticut Department of Consumer Protection and Real Estate
165 Capitol Avenue, Room G8
Hartford, CT 06106
(203) 566-5130

DELAWARE
Delaware Division of Revenue
Carvel State Office Building
820 North French Street
Wilmington, DE 19801

DISTRICT OF COLUMBIA
Department of Consumer and Regulatory Affairs
614 H. Street, N.W.
Washington, D.C. 20001
(202) 727-7100

FLORIDA
Department of Professional Regulation
1940 North Monroe Street
Tallahassee, FL 32399-0762
(904) 488-5189

GEORGIA
Georgia Auctioneers Commission
166 Pryor Street, S.W.
Atlanta, GA 30303
(404) 656-2282

HAWAII
City and County of Honolulu
Department of Finance, Motor Vehicle and Licensing
1455 S. Beretania Street
Honolulu, HI 96814
(808) 973-2810

IDAHO
Real Estate Commission
Statehouse Mail
Boise, ID 83720-6000
(208) 334-3285

ILLINOIS
Office of the Governor
Ronald J. Fagan, State Services Representative
Springfield, IL 62706

INDIANA
Indiana Professional Licensing Agency
1021 Indiana Government Center North
100 North Senate Avenue
Indianapolis, IN 46204-2246
(317) 232-2980

IOWA
Department of Agriculture and Land Stewardship
Wallace Building
Des Moines, IA 50319
(515) 281-6858 or 281-5322

KANSAS
Office of the Attorney General
Second Floor, Kansas Judicial Center
Topeka, KS 66612-1597
(913) 296-2215

KENTUCKY
Kentucky Board of Auctioneers
9112 Leesgate Road, Suite 5
Louisville, KY 40222
(502) 595-4453

Louisiana
Auctioneers Licensing Board
8017 Jefferson Highway, Suite B-3
Baton Rouge, LA 70809
(504) 925-3921

Maine
Department of Professional & Financial Regulation
State House Station #35
Augusta, ME 04333
(207) 582-8723

Maryland
Revenue-generating trader's license required from the local county where auctioneer has place of business. Check with local county licensing agency.

Massachusetts
Division of Standards
One Ashburton Place
Boston, MA 02108
(617) 727-3480

Michigan
Bureau of Occupation and Profession Regulation
Real Estate Board
Post Office Box 30018
Lansing, MI 48909
(517) 373-0490

Minnesota
Application and fees must be made to county auditors throughout state.

Mississippi
Secretary of State
Post Office Box 136
Jackson, MS 39205
(601) 359-1604

Missouri
Auction licenses are issued through the respective county commissions.

Montana
Department of Commerce
Business Licensing Specialist
1424 Ninth Avenue
Helena, MT 59620
(406) 444-3923

Nebraska
Real Estate Commission
Post Office 94667
Lincoln, NE 68509
(502) 471-2004

Nevada
Real Estate Division
1665 Hot Springs Road
Las Vegas, NV 89710
(702) 687-4280

New Hampshire
Board of Auctioneers
Secretary of State's Office,
State House, Room #204
Concord, NH 03301
(603) 271-3242

New Jersey
The state does not require an auctioneer license. However, auction permits and licenses are under local government control. Each jurisdiction sets its own fees and requirements.

New Mexico
Regulation and Licensing Department
725 Saint Michael's Drive
Santa Fe, NM 87504
(505) 827-7006

New York State
New York State Office of Business Permits & Regulatory Assistance
AESOB, 17th Floor
Post Office Box 7027
Albany, NY 12225
(518) 474-8275

North Carolina
North Carolina Auctioneer Licensing Board
Suite 306, Haworth Building
3509 Haworth Drive
Raleigh, NC 27609
(919) 733-2182

North Dakota
Public Service Commission of North Dakota
Grain Elevator Division
State Capitol
Bismarck, ND 58505
(701) 224-4082

Ohio
Ohio Department of Commerce
Division of Licensing
77 S. High Street, 23rd Floor
Columbus, OH 43266-0546
(614) 466-4130

Oklahoma
Governing agencies are established by county treasurers and municipalities.

Oregon
Real Estate Agency
158 12th Street, North East, 2nd Floor
Salem, OR 97310-0240
(503) 378-4170

PENNSYLVANIA
State Board of Auctioneer Examiners
Post Office Box 2649
Harrisburg, PA 17105-2649
(717) 783-3397

RHODE ISLAND
Department of Business Regulation
Division of Licensing and Consumer Protection
233 Richmond Street, Suite #230
Providence, RI 02903-4230
(401) 277-3857

SOUTH CAROLINA
South Carolina Auctioneer's Commission
1200 Main Street, Suite 301
Columbia, SC 29201
(803) 734-1220

SOUTH DAKOTA
Real Estate Commission
Post Office Box 490
Pierre, SD 57501-0490
(605) 773-3600

TENNESSEE
Department of Commerce & Insurance
Auctioneer Commission
500 James Robertson Parkway
Nashville, TN 37243-1152
(615) 741-3236

TEXAS
Texas Department of Licensing & Regulation
Post Office 12157
Austin, TX 78711
(512) 463-3173 or 463-3129

UTAH
Department of Commerce
Post Office Box 45802
Salt Lake City, UT 84145-0802
(801) 530-6955

VERMONT
Secretary of State
Office of Professional Regulation
109 State Street
Montpelier, VT 05609-1106
(802) 828-2191

VIRGINIA
Department of Commerce
Auctioneer Section
3600 W. Broad Street
Richmond, VA 23230-4917
(804) 367-8554

WASHINGTON
Professional Licensing Services
Auctioneer Section
Post Office Box 9020
Olympia, WA 98507-9020
(206) 586-4575

WEST VIRGINIA
West Virginia Department of Agriculture
Marketing & Development Division
East Wing, State Capitol
Charleston, WV 25305
(304) 348-2210

WISCONSIN
Department of Regulation and Licensing
Post Office Box 8935
Madison, WI 53708
(608) 266-5439

WYOMING
Wyoming Attorney General
123 Capitol Building
Cheyenne, WY 82002
(307) 777-7841

> *"The great challenge is to prepare ourselves to enter these doors [of opportunity]."*
> — MARTIN LUTHER KING, JR.

CHAPTER 10

AUCTION SCHOOL 101: INTRODUCTION TO A FAST-PACED WORLD
Getting Educated On The Basics

Auctions are one of the most thrilling and exciting events you can attend today. It is the fastest growing method of sales and marketing in this country. Auctions present one of the best ways to establish fair market value and purchase desired goods.

In this chapter, we will consider the advantages of buying at auction, discuss personal property auctions and review the use of consignment for liquidating an estate.

Why buy at Auction?

All kinds of merchandise, from tobacco and business equipment to real estate and automobiles can be bought or sold at auction. There's just one warning! Once the 'auction bug' has bitten, you'll never get rid of it. You will be hooked forever! Auctions are *not* just for the rich and famous. They can accommodate any pocket book. You set your own price! Many bargains and treasures have been found at auctions. Merchandise generally expected to cost a lot of money, may be found at auction for literally pennies on the dollar. As always, you must do your homework, decide what you are looking for and know when to buy.

Types of Auctions

An auction can contain just about anything known to man. Auctions are simply categorized by the merchandise for sale. There are two general categories: real property and personal property. Here, we will examine the most common types of personal property auctions. A comprehensive list is outlined below:

REAL PROPERTY AUCTIONS	PERSONAL PROPERTY AUCTIONS
REAL ESTATE AUCTIONS (INCLUDING THE SALE OF LAND, CONDOMINIUMS, APARTMENTS, HOUSES, COMMERCIAL BUILDINGS, SHOPPING CENTERS, FARMS, ETC.)	CATTLE & LIVESTOCK
	EXOTIC ANIMALS
	TOBACCO
	AUTO
	MACHINERY & HEAVY EQUIPMENT
	BUSINESS LIQUIDATION
	PERSONAL ESTATE (OR HOUSEHOLD)
	ANTIQUES & COLLECTIBLES
	GOVERNMENT
	FUNDRAISING

All of these auctions are self-explanatory, except for fundraising. A fundraising auction is an event where donated items are auctioned to the highest bidder in order to raise money for charitable organizations and causes. These donations are tax deductible for both the donor and the buyer.

The type of auction you attend will depend on the kind of things you want to buy. For example, attending an estate auction, where the entire contents of a household are presented for sale is a good way to acquire common household goods. General items like furniture, appliances, lawn equipment, pots, pans, linens, and automobiles are found at a personal estate auction.

How to Find an Auction?

The classifieds of your local newspaper are the best place to locate auctions. Simply refer to listings under the "auction" section.

There are special auctions where exclusive types of items are sold. These sales will be listed under "auctions," as well as, the specialized heading of the classifieds. For example, if an auction company is having a business liquidation, it will be listed under "auction," as well as, "business equipment." Estates with an extensive amount of antiques may be listed under the "antiques" section

AUCTION 101: INTRODUCTION TO A FAST-PACED WORLD

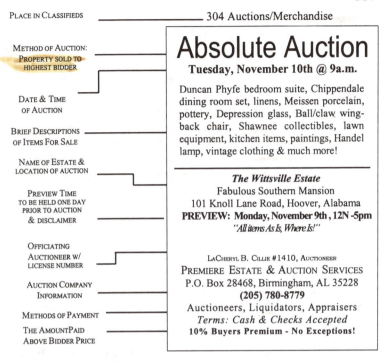

also. The best days to check the paper for sales are Thursday, Friday, and Sunday since most auctions are held on weekends.

The advertisement will contain basic information including the name of the estate or its owners, the location, date, time of previews (days or hours), methods of payment, a brief description of items, license number of auctioneer (if this is a state requirement), phone number of auction company, disclaimers, terms and conditions of sale. Advertisements don't always list all of the items in the sale and often will end in such phrases as... " *much more, or items too numerous to list.*"

If the auction is **absolute** (which means each item goes to the highest bidder regardless of the price), it will be boldly listed in the ad. If "absolute" is not listed in the ad, then you should assume there is a **reserve** on some, if not all, of the items in the sale. A reserve means that the owners or heirs have set a minimum selling price for certain items.

Most auction companies apply a **buyer's premium**, and it will usually be listed in the ad. If the buyer's premium is 10%, you will pay 10% above your bidding price. Let's say your bid is $100, then you will pay $110 for your item.

You should also be aware of disclaimers on ads that express: *"as is, where is."* This is a common phrase used by auction companies to inform their buying clients that there is no guarantee on the condition of merchandise and that they buyer is responsible for removing any purchased merchandise from the auction premises.

Another important disclaimer to take note of outlines that *"statements made the day of sale by auctioneer company take precedence over any statement made prior to the sale."* This simply means that whatever the auctioneer outlines the day of the sale outweighs any other information stated prior to the auction day.

Auction Brochures

Auction companies have extensive mailing lists. It is a good idea to contact the auctioneer or auction company and request a brochure of sales items prior to the auction.

Usually the auction company will mail a brochure or flyer announcement a week to ten days prior to sale. The brochure will contain essentially the same information as stated in the newspaper ad. However, brochures and flyers go a step further, usually containing black and white photos or color pictures. With the brochure, you will learn more details about the items for sale. A description is usually given of specialty items. For example, an antique, Chippendale chair might read *"Cherry Chippendale Style Chair Circa 1895."* The circa simply means 'year dated.' If there is any provenance (or ownership information) about a piece, it will be fully described.

Also, listed in the brochure will be a disclaimer, *'Sold As Is, Where Is.'* This simply means, *"what you see is what you get!"* Once the auction gavel goes down and *"Sold!"* is the auctioneers' cry — the sales item belongs to you and it is your sole responsibility.

Being a part of the mailing list will give you a chance to do your homework prior to the preview (the time designated for buyers to review merchandise prior to sale). This is your best opportunity to ask any questions of the auctioneer about any item listed in the brochure.

Brochures will also let you know about inclement

weather and if the auction will continue rain or shine. This is an important factor since auctions can last several hours or days depending on the number of items to be sold.

Word of Mouth

It is good to begin conversations with other auction goers as you attend auctions and recognize familiar faces. People who attend auctions regularly will be on several mailing lists and will have information about all types of upcoming auction events. Forming new friendships will also make it a more enjoyable way to shop and spend the day. So, be engaging, mingle among the crowd and keep a listening ear tuned. The information shared will prove to be invaluable.

Publications

The *Antique Trader* and *The Maine Antique Digest* are two antique and collectible trade newspapers that list auctions nationwide. The ads are normally large and will usually contain photos of items in the sale. Most advertised auctions are listed two weeks prior to sale. Auctions are listed according to region. The newspapers are published weekly. Yearly subscriptions are available

It is not uncommon for collectors to travel thousands of miles to buy a particular piece. Groups of collectors form membership clubs and list auctions in their respective newsletters as well. Begin your subscriptions with these trade magazines:

Antique Trader
Post Office Box 1050
Dubuque, IA 52004-1050
One-year subscription, $35 for 52 weekly issues

The Maine Antique Digest
P.O. Box 1429
Waldboro, ME 04572
1-207-832-4888
Published monthly, at $29 for an annual subscription

Legal Newspapers

Both legal newspapers and legal sections in local newspapers give notice of estate sales, bankruptcies, real estate auctions and business liquidations. You will also find announcements of auto auctions, machinery sales and adoptions. Check around your local community for a legal publication that you can subscribe to.

Government & Corporate Auctions

Government auctions are probably the largest auctions held in the United States. The General Services Administration (GSA) is a federal agency created to handle the disposal of all government surplus. Anything the government owns finds it's way to auction at some point. This is done through live auctions, as well as, by absentee bidding via mail. The government has separate mailing lists based on your area of interest. Refer to the ten GSA regions listed below to be placed on the mailing list. Write directly to the GSA, Director of Personal Property Division or GSA, Director of Real Property at the address in your region.

GSA Mailing List
Personal Property Division

REGION 1: Connecticut, Maine, Massachusetts, New Hampshire, Rhode Island, Vermont: *John W. McCormack Post Office and Courthouse Boston, MA 02109*

REGION 2: New York, New Jersey, Puerto Rico, Virgin Islands: *26 Federal Plaza, New York, NY 10007*

REGION 3: District of Columbia, Delaware, Maryland, Pennsylvania, Virginia, West Virginia: *7th and D Streets SW, Washington, DC 20407*

REGION 4: Alabama, Florida, Georgia, Kentucky, Mississippi, North Carolina, South Carolina, Tennessee: *1776 Peachtree Street, NW Atlanta, GA 30309*

REGION 5: Illinois, Indiana, Michigan, Minnesota, Ohio, Wisconsin: *230 South Dearborn St. Chicago, IL 60604*

REGION 6: Iowa, Kansas, Missouri, Nebraska: *1500 East Bannister Rd. Kansas City, MO 64131*

REGION 7: Arkansas, Louisiana, New Mexico, Oklahoma, Texas: *819 Taylor St. Forth Worth, TX 76102*

REGION 8: Colorado, Montana, North Dakota, South Dakota, Utah, Wyoming: *Denver Federal Center Bldg. 41 Denver, CO 80225*

REGION 9: American Samoa, Arizona, California, Guam, Hawaii, Nevada, the Trust Territory of the Pacific Islands: *525 Market Street, San Francisco, CA 94105*

REGION 10: Alaska, Idaho, Oregon, Washington: *GSA, Auburn, WA 98002*

Department of Defense
Property Disposal Division

REGION 1: DPDR-Columbus, Attn: *DPDR-CMB 3900 E. Broad St. Columbus, OH 43215*

REGION 2: DPDR-MMB *2163 Airways Blvd Memphis, TN 38114*

REGION 3: DPDR-OMB *500 W. 12th Street Ogden, UT 84401*

REAL ESTATE: *Department of Defense, Surplus Property Sales, Post Office Box 1370 Battle Creek, MI 49016*

Governmental agencies such as the Internal Revenue Services, U.S. Marshall, the U.S. Postal Service and U.S. Customs also hold auctions from time to time. Your local classifieds would be the place to look for their advertised sales under "auction."

State and city governments may also dispose of property by the auction method. Advertisement can be found in the newspaper. Other public agencies in your area that may dispose of merchandise via auction include the local police department, state universities, utility companies and major supply corporations. A call to someone in the purchasing department of these businesses and institutions will provide you information on upcoming auction sales. Be sure to ask about their mailing list.

Consignments: The Selling Advantage

Auctioneers and auction houses will charge a fee or percentage for items consigned or entrusted to them for sale. For an additional fee, most companies will allow you to place a minimum bid on the item. In the event your piece doesn't sell, they may charge a buy-back fee, assuming you have a reserve on the item. Consigned items may contain anything from automobiles to xylophones.

Consignment sales can include one item or an entire group. For more information on locating consignment companies, check your local yellow pages, under "auction houses" or "auctioneers."

When an estate needs to be liquidated, an auction of the entire estate may be a good choice. The auctioneer will host the sale and often negotiate with the owner on who will pay for advertising. The auction company will provide set up and cleanup labor. The hired company will always do their best for you. The bottom line guarantees it. The more you make, the more they make!

The use of auctions as a way of exchanging goods, has experienced a recent revival in American society. Auctions bring interested buyers in one location—at one time—to bid on all the things they are looking for. Fair market value is always established in this setting.

You can be reasonably assured that all of your items will be sold the day of auction. As the owner, you will have no additional concern for these items. Auction sales really do accelerate the marketing process. When advertised and done properly, auctions will command the highest price for your merchandise. The element of theatrics, combined with competition, serves to increase the price on sales items.

"Risks, big and small, are the way those of us not born to wealth can pursue it and achieve success."
CLARENCE PAGE

CHAPTER 11

ADVANCED TRAINING: DEVELOPING STRATEGIES FOR AUCTION
Mental Preparation for Auction Action

Now that you've had a brief introduction to the fast-paced world of auctions. You'll need to follow these basic strategies to help you stay mentally prepared for action in this arena. The following preparation notes will bring out the savvy shopper in you and keep you from those underlying auction pitfalls.

Strategy #1: Attend a few auctions prior to your first bid. Try to attend a few auctions before you participate in the bidding process. Observe procedures and check out the crowd. Learn to follow the bidding strategies used by winning bidders. Some think that showing no sign of excitability until final bid works best. Others choose to begin the bid process with fervency and remain in 'high gear' until the end. After watching the different personalities and approaches, determine the method that is most conducive to your style and comfort. Then be prepared to go for it!

Strategy #2: Always preview before buying at auction. At each auction there will be hundreds of items to choose from. While the auctioneer will have an expertise on most things, he will not know everything about each item. He will at least have a clue of what is the fair market value.

This is especially true with general estate auctions, because there are so many different items.

Specialty auctions (where only a certain type of merchandise is sold) can pull on your wallet. Not only will the auctioneer know what the item is, but so will the rest of the crowd. Be prepared for a fight, particularly if an item is a rare and valuable piece. The motto is simple, "May the best man or woman win!"

In every situation, do your homework. Be knowledgeable of the prevailing price of an item, along with its rating in terms of provenance, condition, rarity, supply and demand. Set a price in your mind based on your research. Do not deviate from that price unless you are emotionally and financially prepared to do so.

When doing your homework, bring along necessary tools such as a jeweler's loupe (magnifying glass), black light, tape measure and a note pad. If a piece of fine porcelain is in the auction, bring a pocket guide with marks to check authenticity. If you are looking at jewelry consider how markings for gold and silver are noted. Gold will be indicated by the karat. The markings are 9K, 10K, 14K, 15K, 18K 22K and 24K. If the markings are 9K or 15K, they represent older pieces and are very valuable. Sterling silver which is 925 parts of 1000 will be marked by 925, STG, Sterling, or Silver. To test for real pearls, wipe them thoroughly then place them in your mouth and bite down. If they are gritty, you may have a real set of pearls in your hands. If the pearls are smooth, they are probably fake. Again, be sure to maintain your set price based on your homework.

Strategy # 3: Remember everyone is potential competition. Be leery of folks who go on about how terrible a item is during the auction preview period. These same people are usually the ones who will out bid everyone! It is their attempt to sway you in your bid by leaking false or negative information.

The savvy buyer will often be seen and not heard. He or she will immediately recognize an item as a great buy and fail to mention it to anyone until the winning bid is achieved. It's a "quiet revolution" of wit and strategy. So, be on the lookout for these diverse kinds of bidding tactics. An auction is a price war. Essentially everyone is a potential competition.

Strategy #4: Pay close attention to descriptions of merchandise. Listen very carefully to the auctioneer's description of the merchandise. Some auctioneers will suggest that an item is something that it simply is not. This may be unintentional, but it won't matter once you're the owner. Remember that all items are sold "as is." Essentially, what you see is what you get! By the same token, the auctioneer may not know the exact quality or fuller background of a piece. In that instance, just sit back and wait. Always remain calm, cool and collected. When moving in for the kill, grin only in your shoes and hide those sweaty palms!

Rely on your knowledge when analyzing descriptions. You should be able to make intelligent decisions from your research about the authenticity of merchandise. This will enable you to see right through the jargon. Instinctively, you will know whether a horn is being tooted too much or not enough.

Strategy #5: Set your $pending limit and hold firm. Once you have carefully examined the items you are interested in, make a mental note or even jot down on a note pad the top amount you are willing to spend. Then hold fast to it! If you decide there is room beyond this limit, then move ahead accordingly. Otherwise, keep calm and don't let emotional ploys cause you to spend more than you intend to or can reasonably afford.

Strategy #6: Be an active listener. Watch the auctioneer and observe who is bidding. Remain an active listener while you are reviewing and considering all merchandise. Meanwhile, the bidding process will continue rapidly around you. If you are involved in the process maintain good listening skills. Be careful not to raise your own bid. Certainly, most honest auctioneers will let you know he has you "in" and will began asking someone else for the next higher bid. There are some that will allow you to raise your own bid and you end up bidding against yourself. This is auction suicide, so pay close attention.

If a piece is up for bid and you need a second look, the auctioneer will often let you take a quick glance. Motion one of the ringmen helping with the sale. He will bring a piece to you for a closer examination. Stay alert to the bidding process while you are looking.

Strategy #7: Don't hesitate to ask questions. In the heat of buying passion, the bidding process can get somewhat confusing. If you feel out of control, simply stop and collect yourself. Don't hesitate to ask appropriate questions of the ringman about the process. It's okay to back out for a moment. I guarantee the ringmen will be watching if you have bid or shown any signs of interest. Don't be nervous once you enter back into the bidding. Have confidence that you know what you want and how to maneuver. Auctions are for those with quick wit and solid thoughts. So pace yourself and don't be afraid to slow down and ask questions.

Strategy #8: Be watchful for signs of dishonesty or manipulation. If you feel that dishonest or illegal tactics are being used to illicit bids, then this not the auction for you! For example, some companies will accept phone (or absentee) bids. Judge the authenticity of such bids from the overall reputation of the auction company. Dishonest auctioneers may use this as a ploy to increase bids. On the other hand, such bids do exist and are honestly done throughout the country. Buyers who cannot attend an auction will often send in an absentee bid. They may even be allowed to phone in their bids. Remember that auction companies advertise in trade magazines and send brochures across the continental United States. It's just a necessary precaution, to make sure all sales are performed with integrity.

Strategy #9: Stay cool— when your desired item comes up for bid. Auctions are emotionally charged and fast-paced. Buyer competition can get heated and fierce. Make sure you wave your number in the air when interested in bidding. If you are not noticed, get the attention of the ringmen and they will keep a watchful eye on you. Once your first bid is accepted, put your number down until someone else has bid. This is important, so that you will not bid against yourself. The most critical advice here is to: *keep a level head during the bidding process.* Remember that events are going to be moving fast, the noise levels will be extremely high and the buying energy pretty intense. If a buying ego takes over, you will pay more for an item than it is worth. So, make sure you have your prices jotted down and a clear strategy outlined to successfully maneuver you through the process.

==The critical element is composure.== You may want that Hepplewhite sideboard to match your dining room table and chairs *really* bad, but don't mortgage the house to get it! Stay cool! If you become prematurely attached to an item, your buying reason will be off balance. Again, set a price limit for yourself and give it your best shot!

> *"I was cool and perfectly at ease. I never had any doubts of the outcome."*
> JACK JOHNSON, C. 1920

CHAPTER 12

AUCTION DAY: MANEUVERING WITH SKILL & CONFIDENCE
Get Ready For The Time of Your Life!

Buyer Beware! This is true for most auctions. If you are not careful, you can innocently 'lose your shirt'. Avoiding this dilemma takes maneuvering with skill and confidence. In this chapter, we will get you ready for a successful time in the auction arena.

The Auction Preview

Always attend the auction preview - whether it is held several days before the auction or several hours prior to the sale. During this time you will be able to examine the sales items carefully. For an estate auction, you can expect at least three bedrooms, kitchen, dining room, living room, den, bathroom, and garage area. Common household items will fill each room for your viewing pleasure.

Be sure to bring along tools that will aid in your research, like a jeweler's loupe (magnifying glass), price guides[12], black light (to reveal cracks in porcelain), tape measure and a note pad. These instruments of the trade will help you determine the condition of items and enable you to enter the bidding process as an informed buyer. Applying these preview strategies will make your attendance at auction more fruitful and rewarding. Always proceed with caution when bidding on items you have not previewed! Overall, buying at auction should prove to be a great savings over most retail prices.

Going To Auction

BIDDING NUMBER

325

USE THIS CARD TO BID

For your protection
do not Lose this number.
All guarantees are between
Buyer and Seller.
All purchases must be settled
for today. 10% Buyer's Premium.

No items to be removed until settled for.
Not responsible in case of accidents on premises.

You are responsible
for your own items
after making purchase

Bidder Card

On the day of auction, rise and shine early! Make sure to bring a note pad along to jot down the items you're interested in. Regardless of the type of auction you attend, they will all follow a similar format. Each will consist of a large or small gathering of eager buyers anxiously waiting for show time.

Prior to the opening of the auction, you must go through the bidder registration line. Have your drivers' license available because it is required for legal identification. Here, you will receive a catalog (listing the items for sale) and a bidder card or paddle (with your buyer number). In order to buy at any auction, you must have this bidder card. You can't participate without it! Make sure you read thoroughly over the information on the bidder card. If there is a buyer's premium, it will usually be listed here. For example:

If the buyer's premium is 10%, you will pay 10% above your bidding price. Let's say your bid is $100, then you will pay $110 for your item.

After reading the bidder card, you will sign your name and address to enter a formal contract outlining the rules of conduct. This contract simply makes you responsible for any bids made to your buyer number and assures the auction company that you will accept items *"as is."* Also included, may be a disclaimer stating that *"whatever announcements made by the auctioneer on the day of sale, take precedence over any previous announcements."* In other words, announcements made the day of sale outweigh any previous claims you may have heard.

Once this process is complete, you are ready for auction!

Auction Day: Maneuvering With Skill & Confidence

Quickly look over any last minute items once again. The catalog will list the items for sale by name and lot number. A lot number is the inventory number assigned to every item to be sold at auction. Some auctions proceed with the sale of items in strict numerical order (from lowest to highest) and others deviate.

Once you have noted your items of interest, check out concessions for your favorite foods. Most auction companies sell refreshments and light food items such as hot dogs, sodas, pickles, cakes, pies, hamburger, and barbecue. Once you've had a snack, take a seat. The show is about to begin.

The auction will start with the auctioneer making a few announcements about terms and conditions of sale. If there are any noted changes, he will make them at this time. The auctioneer will advise you of your buying rights and inform you that the auction is being video taped. Many auctions are taped in case bidding discrepancies arise. With the use of video, the auctioneer can easily rely on a 'play back' to address disagreements. The clerk, ringmen, cashier and others assisting the auctioneer will then be introduced. Their various duties are as follows:

- Clerk – Records winning bidder numbers and the official amount of items sold.
- Ringmen – Represents an 'extra set of eyes' for the auctioneer in accepting bids.
- Cashier – Receives payment for merchandise and provides a receipt at check out.
- Assisting Auctioneers – Provide relief (or breaks) for the officiating auctioneer.

You will also receive verbal instructions on payment and pickup procedures. The auctioneer will inform you on the most common ways bids are accepted. He or she will dismiss the rumors of bidding by rubbing your nose, scratching your head, fanning flies, or any other nonsense. Bids are accepted when you lift a bidder card in the air, nod your head to acknowledge a bid or clearly raise your hand to signify bidding interest. With all of the announcements made, a seasoned auctioneer will proceed to warm up the crowd with a little humor or fast chant jargon. Again, I must warn you about the auction bug.

Once you've been bit, it never lets go! But, oh what fun it is! Now, it's auction time. The auctioneer will start with the lot number and description of the first item. He will proceed to solicit bids something like this:

"We begin our auction today with item #001 in your catalog. It is a, turn of the century, Handel lamp. Do I hear a bid of $500, $500, do I hear a bid of five hundred dollars...."

The bid is accepted if someone in the crowd waives his hand, or the ringman, answers "Yes!" This means someone has agreed to that amount. The auctioneer then raises the bid, and it is accepted again.

"I see a $1,000, where is $1100 for the Handel lamp. I see $1100!"

He will continue raising the bid in incremental steps until the excitement climaxes and bidding ceases. At the sound of the highest bid, the auctioneer will cry "Sold!" and the gavel will sound. At this point, the amount and bidder number is announced:

"This beautiful turn of the century Handel lamp is sold for $1200 to bidder #75. Congratulations, sir!"

The auction will proceed with the next item and the next until all items are sold. Auctions go very fast and are full of energy. Many would agree it is emotionally charged and competition is often fierce.

Make sure you wave your number in the air when interested in bidding. If you are not noticed, get the attention of the ringmen. Once they know

Sterling silver sherberts tagged with lot #322 waiting to be sold at auction.

you are interested, they will keep an eye on you. After your first bid is accepted, put your number down until someone else has bid. Then proceed to bid again when you are ready. This will keep you from bidding against yourself. Try to keep a level head during this process. Remember these things are emotionally charged! Be careful, because a buying ego will make you pay 3 to 4 times what an item is worth. Develop your own bidding strategies prior to auction and never let them see you sweat! Keep in mind, the auctioneer wants to get as much as he or she possibly can on each item. So, stay cool! If you don't, your bidding will be swayed and manipulated. Avoid taking a mental stance against a competing bidder like, *"They will not have this!"* Once an emotionally charged contest is detected, the auctioneer will ride the wave. There will literally be no end until every dollar is realized. The highly charged atmosphere will continue with this same fervor until all items are sold.

You need to define your price limits prior to bidding and try to stay within that range. Make sure you jot down lot numbers of items purchased and the amounts. A good way to keep things straight is to circle the lot number on your catalog and write your winning bid amount beside it. This will help you maintain clear records. Do not hesitate to inform the cashier of any errors. With all the theatrics and high noise levels - it may be possible for a cashier to record your bid inaccurately. So, be very mindful of what you bid.

1907 signed chandelier purchased at auction, value $600-$1200
Photo by: Leon Stoudemire

When the auction is over, you will need to go to the cashier checkout and pay for your things. Once the cashier clears your purchases and gives you a receipt, proceed to the merchandise pick-up table to receive your goods. Merchandise will not be released without this receipt, so hold on to it. Be sure to keep up with your purchases once you claim them. The auction company will not be responsible for any lost or stolen items. So it may be a good idea to secure smaller items purchased and keep them within your sight. Unfortunately, everyone at the auction is not always honest. Also be careful not to break purchased items, because returns are not permitted. If newspaper is provided, wrap and store your items well. At the end of the day, take your purchases home and enjoy your new "riches" with your family. You will have the satisfying feeling of having maneuvered with skill and confidence in this historical sales arena.

Madame Auctioneer, LaCheryl Cillie showing a winning smile while posing with auction colleagues during her apprenticeship. To date, she is the first African-American, male or female, to become a licensed auctioneer in the State of Alabama. *Photo by Leon Stoudemire.*

---

[12] Check out *Shroeder's Antiques Price Guide 1997* (Collector Books) and *Warman's Americana & Collectibles—7th Edition* (Krause Publications).

PART V

The Estate Sale: On Your Mark, Get Set, Ready, Go!

> *"The time has come when you must act for yourselves".*
> HENRY HIGHLAND GARNET, 1865

CHAPTER 13

ATTENDING THE ESTATE SALE
Early Bird Gets The Goods!

Estate sales are an excellent source for locating all kinds of valuable merchandise, from antique furniture and household appliances to lawn equipment and automobiles. Estate sales are also commonly referred to as *tagged sales*. They are generally more formal and organized than your average garage or yard sale, because they are hosted and run by professionals.

A tag sale conductor is an estate expert who organizes the sales event and "tags" the items for purchase. If the estate contains valuable antiques or collectibles, the conductor will provide a general appraisal and assign a price accordingly.

As you read through this chapter, you find a few terrific treasures we have purchased at auctions and estate sales; along with the approximate amount paid for each item and an estimate of its worth.

Estate (tagged) Sales vs. Estate Auctions
An estate is a vast collection of one's life possessions. So an estate sale often contains everything imaginable! There are a surprising number of people who collect everything, keep everything, buy everything and never use it! Therefore, these sales often contain merchandise never used. Many contain jewelry, business equipment, kitchenware, linens, clothing, books, and much more.

Humpback trunk circa 1850 to 1890, worth $150 - $375. Photo: Leon Stoudemire

Estate (tagged) sales and estate auctions and have many similarities. Both result in a comprehensive inventory and formal appraisal in the liquidation of personal property. In the tag sale, the conductor appraises and sets prices. Once a price is set, it generally cannot be negotiated. In the estate auction, the bidding audience establishes individual pricing. There is no preview day with a tag sale. On the other hand, estate auctions always allow merchandise inspection and preview times. With either sale, bargains can be found and magnificent treasures are available.

Although there are noted differences between tag sales and auctions, the sale of merchandise is the common result. There are advantages and disadvantages in either situation. However, both prove to be excellent ways to buy and sell merchandise.

Common Reasons Why Estate Sales Are Held

There are several reasons why an estate is sold. The most common reason is the disposal of personal property after death. Heirs are often left with a responsibility to liquidate a loved one's residential estate, in order to pay outstanding debts. Too, elderly persons with failing health will often sell their estate to move in with relatives or relocate to a retirement home.

An estate sale can also take place when a homeowner relocates to another state or moves out of the country. Finally, churches and other non-profit organizations will sometimes inherit an estate from a wealthy donor and need to liquidate their new assets.

Where To Find Sales

Tag sales are also advertised in the classified section of your local newspaper, usually under the heading of "garage sales." The words "estate sale" will boldly appear in the ad. The newspaper ad will appear one to three days prior to sale. It will list all of the pertinent information including date, time, location, terms & conditions, and conductor's name. Most sales are held on Friday and Saturday or Saturday and Sunday from early morning to mid afternoon, generally from 9 a.m. to 3 p.m.

If there are antiques or collectibles in the sale, the ad will describe them briefly. Often, the conductor will list his or her name at the beginning or end of the ad. This is done because many conductors have a general following. If the estate belongs to a well-known collector or dealer in the area, that person's name will also be mentioned.

Queen Anne Bed, part of bedroom suite purchased by author, LaCheryl Cillie in 1984 for $900. Includes nightstand, dresser and chest of drawers, worth $3000. Photo by Leon Stoudemire

Pre-Sales (Tag Sale)

With certain estates a pre-sale will be held for family and friends prior to the public sale. An experienced tag sale conductor will already have a pre-sale call list. This list includes the names of buyers who have indicated a serious search for a particular item, along with personal friends and colleagues. A good way to get on this call list is to attend sales often, develop a buying relationship with the conductor or simply ask to be included on the list. All conductors do not hold a pre-sale in every circumstance.

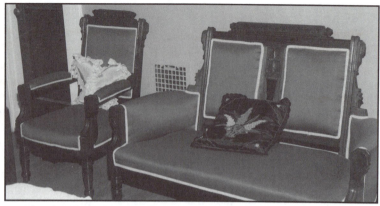

Victorian Eastlake parlor set, purchased for $275, worth $695-$995

Preparation Prior to Sale

Prior to attending a pre-sale or public sale, it is very important to research the items listed in the ad. If you are interested in a particular item, take the time to determine its value. For example, if a Kenmore Range is advertised, take a trip to Sears to price a new one. Then formulate a good buying price in your notes for the used appliance.

For antiques and collectibles, visit antique shops and look in price guides. These guides are a great source of wisdom and knowledge. You certainly should not expect to pay more than the book value for any item.

As mentioned earlier, tag sales do not have preview days like auctions. So, you need to be prepared prior to attending the sale because you may not get a second look at that particular item. Remember to bring your own shopping bags, jewelry loupes, magnifying glasses, pocket guides, and any other tools necessary to make an educated decision about your purchases. Be sure to consider the transportation of larger items you buy at a sale. Having access to a truck is always helpful.

Attending An Estate Sale

Most tag sales start around 8 or 9 a.m. Buyers come from near and far, as the popularity of these sales continues to increase. So, arrive early to secure your place at the head of the line. Numbers are given to attendees upon arrival. Lower numbers are ideal, because buyers can enter the house first. Since the items are already tagged, people may pick items up quickly as they enter the house. If you

ATTENDING THE ESTATE SALE   141

see something you want, and it's small, go ahead and hold on to it. Generally, you will have to peel the price tag from larger items (such as, furniture, appliances, large rugs, and mirrors) when you want to buy them. Do not assume that you have time to think about those obvious deals. Chances are there are twenty other people who think the same way.

Estate sales are one of the major sources of acquiring merchandise for collectors, antique dealers, and flea market vendors. They will be on the move! So if you want it, pick it up the first time or it may not be there when you return. After you have gone through the rooms in the house, ask if there is a garage or basement. These areas are usually full of great finds too.

Submitting Silent Bids On Sales Items

You may have questions about the price of a large ticket item, like a boat or automobile. Ask the host if **silent bids** will be accepted on any items that do not sell the first day as priced. A silent bid is simply your written offer on a particular sale item.

On the second day of the sale some items may be sold for half price. Some hosts will allow you to leave a silent bid for more than half the price in order to secure the item. This opportunity is extended to all buyers in attendance. The highest bidder wins. In the event your bid is the highest, you will receive a call later that evening from the sale conductor. The following day you must claim your item before the sale is over. Otherwise, it will be sold to the next highest bidder or for half price.

Tiger-oak Lady's Desk, purchased for $325, worth $595 - $995.
Photo: Leon Stoudemire

Payment for Goods

Most conductors accept cash and checks drawn on local banks. A driver's license will be needed to validate your information. As certain conductors get to know you, a license will probably not be required. If checks will not be accepted, it will be mentioned in the initial advertisement. Otherwise, it is safe to assume that checks are welcomed. Major credit cards, however, are not normally accepted.

Removal of Sales Items

When purchasing a large item that requires a truck for transporting, it is wise to plan ahead. Estate sale companies are **pretty** strict about this. You will need to remove your items during the time allotted for the sale. In some instances, later arrangements can be made. However, do not count on this. Once you purchase an item it becomes your sole responsibility. Any damage or theft that may occur as a result of an item being left unattended is yours. So plan to promptly remove your merchandise.

A Note Of Departure

Before departing a sale, always inquire about future sale dates. If you have special interest in particular items, be sure to inform the sales conductor. You will be asked to sign a call list indicating your interests. If your desired item is acquired by the sales company, expect to be contacted by phone or mail. Also ask to be included on the conductor's pre-sale list for upcoming estate sales.

Black Italian wash stand, purchased for $195, worth $795 - $1100.

> *"Take the cash, forget the credit."*
> - Coleman Young, *Detroit Monthly*, 1981

CHAPTER 14

GETTING INTO THE SALES BUSINESS
Liquidating Property Is Easier Than You Think

It is a fact of life that we are born to die. Growing up in church as a child, I often heard the minister remind us that "we brought nothing into to this world and it is certain we will carry nothing out." This is a sober reality.

Because of this truth, it is quite possible that we will be left with a relative's personal property to dispose of. If you are unsure about the value of particular items, it makes good economic sense to obtain the assistance of a auctioneer or tag sale conductor. Initially, they will help you determine whether a formal auction or estate sale is best.

These professionals make it part of their continuing education to become very knowledgeable about a wide range of items. If it is the estate of an older relative, there may be valuable items such as antique and collectibles.

Whether a partial or complete liquidation of the estate is called for, their insights will bring peace of mind and the highest possible amount for the merchandise.

A Word About Dealers and Collectors

Beware that there are dealers and collectors who specialize in all sorts of merchandise from paper goods and autographs, to furniture and glassware. You name it! They would just love for you to have an informal garage sale or take a dumping trip to the local thrift store. Collectors know the value of the items they collect. Do you think they would inform you that your Depression glass is worth more than $.50 cents? If your answer is no, then you are absolutely correct! They will buy all that you have for fifty cents, and ask to see what else you are selling.

Believe me, dealers and collectors are waiting for families, just like yours, to depart with their *historical riches*. These folks have booths at flea market, antique malls and trade shows. They are constantly looking for new merchandise to fill these spaces.

Having a formal estate sale makes better sense. At least you will have a better chance of getting a good price for all of your valuable pieces. The auctioneer and tag sale conductor will know what the going market price is for most items. This will definitely minimize your getting taken advantage of.

Hiring An Auctioneer or Tag Sale Conductor

When contemplating a formal liquidation sale, ask the attorney handling the estate to recommend someone with experience that meets your specific needs. If you don't have an attorney, look in the yellow pages under auctions, auctioneers, estate sales, or appraisals. Appraisers assess the value of personal property and often handle sales for the courts and individual attorneys.

Duncan Phyfe sideboard holds silver and glassware tagged for an estate sale. An African-American family inherited this estate from an older relative, and realized in excess of $20,000 from the furnishings alone.

Victorian marble-top table with Occupied Japan porcelain, carnival glass, and 'Gone With the Wind' lamp (reproduction) displayed at recent estate sale.

As with any major decision, handle it with care. Be sure to ask how familiar they are with your type of personal property. Obtain references and fee schedules prior to making a decision. Fees to hire these professionals generally range from 3% to 33 1/3% based on the type of merchandise sold. Be ready to negotiate, but don't be unreasonable. Included in that fee will be setup, cleanup, sale crew and advertising. The sales company will assume total responsibility for monies paid, checks written, theft of property, and damage to property. Most auctioneers and tag sale conductors have extensive mailing list and a large following of people hungry for your merchandise.

Hosting a personal property sale is labor intensive, whether auctioned or tagged. If a sale is held at a residence, cleaning and set-up are essential. The way the items are organized and arranged may effect the price. However, having a sale at the house where a person lived increases the price 20 to 30%. There is something about seeing an item just as the owner left it, which excites the buying public. Somehow, it makes them feel good or connected to that individual. This produces a receptive attitude that is reflected in their willingness to purchase. Psychologically, they almost feel it is their duty to buy. I have seen this over and over again with both tagged and auction sales.

On the contrary, removing an item from its original "home site" diminishes its value in the eyes of the buyer. A little dust and a hint of musty smells yields good results. Surprisingly, the more dust, the greater the desire to own the piece. This is do in part to the fact that it makes the age of the item seem more believable.

Average household items overlooked by most people which are excellent sale items include like pots, pans, dishes, appliances, cleaning supplies, sheets, towels, spreads, can goods (Yes, cleaners and can goods). To draw people to your sale, the sale conductor will list these simple, yet important facts in the ad. Obviously, the more money obtained from the sale, the better 'pay day' for the auctioneer or tag sale conductor! Hosting successful tagged or auction sales relies greatly on the "word of mouth" as its advertising. If the sales conductor does a good job, you will tell five other people. If they do a lousy job, you will tell ten. So, they are highly motivated.

Assessing Your Estate

The decision to have a sale will depend upon many of the factors surrounding the estate. If liquidation is necessary, and desired, it is best to hire a professional. Keep the following things in mind as you seek to liquidate the entire contents of an estate:

- Make sure you have 'enough' to sell beforehand. Removing items before a professional assessment, may decrease your chances of having a successful sale.
- Always leave merchandise in place and 'as it sits' throughout the estate.
- Allow the professional to see *all* of the items that will be displayed for sale. Remember, everything from canned goods to cleaning supplies is important.

Following an initial assessment, you will be advised on if you have an estate with good sales potential. This will save you the time and effort of fooling with liquidation. The sheet on the following page represent a sample inventory list that would be used by a sale conductor, to determine the value of various items in an estate.

In a final analysis, the auctioneer or tag sale conductor will have done all of the work and you will be the recipient of a hefty sum!

PREMIERE ESTATE AND AUCTION SERVICE,
P. O. BOX 28468, BIRMINGHAM, AL 35228, (205) 780-8779

ESTATE INVENTORY
OF
MINNIE MAE JONES

KITCHEN

Kenmore gas stove, white, excellent condition, value: $325.

Kenmore side-by-side, frost-free, white refrigerator excellent condition, value: $500.

5-piece chrome dinnette set, 1950's, red, good condition, value: $375.

Assorted pots and pans, dishes, flatware, dishcloths, etc., good condition, value: $500.

Assorted pictures on wall (4), decorative plates (4), good condition, value: $250.

Assorted canned goods and other non-perishable food items, cleaning supplies and utensils, value: $200.

Small appliances, including toasters, mixers, can opener, microwave, percolator/coffee pot, value: $400.

LIVING ROOM

Three (3) Piece Victorian parlor set, late 1870's, new upholstery, good condition, value $2800.

Three (3) Marble-top Victorian tables, reproduction, 1940's, good condition, value: $395 each.

Assorted pictures on wall (4), fair, value: $200.

Brice-a-brac: pottery, porcelain, and cut-glass, good condition, value: $500.

Two (2) Gone-with-the-wind parlor lamps, hand-painted shades, reproduction, 1930's, excellent condition, value: $375 each.

Page Two: Minnie Mae Jones Estate
July, 14, 1997
Conducted By: LaCheryl Cillie

DINING ROOM

9-Piece Duncan Phyfe dining room suite with shield-back chairs, reproduction,1940's, excellent condition, value: $3500.
Sterling Silver 12-piece place setting flatware, Gorham, Strasbourg pattern, excellent, $3600.
12-Piece place setting of Lenox Autumn pattern fine china, excellent condition, value: $3000.
12 Gorham goblets, cherrywood pattern, excellent condition, value: $450.

BEDROOM #1

4-Piece Queen Anne 4 poster cherry bedroom suite, reproduction 1980's, good condition, value: $1100.
Pictures (4) on bedroom walls, fair, value: $400.
Wing-chair, blue, cabriole legs, good condition, value: $250.

BEDROOM #2

4-Piece Duncan Phye Mahogany bedroom suite, reproduction 1940s, good condition, value: $2500.
Slipper chair, Damask upholstery, good condition, value: $175.

LINENS

Assorted bedspreads, blankets, sheets, towels, pillows, pillowcases, quilts, bath rugs, and shower curtains, good to fair, value: $500.

LaCheryl Cillie
LACHERYL CILLIE, AUCTIONEER, AL LIC. #1410

July 14, 1997
DATE OF INVENTORY

PLEASE NOTE: This is not an official appraisal. The hand-written inventory represents a general survey of the above-mentioned estate by the auctioneer here signed. If an official appraisal is deemed necessary, it will be provided upon request.

PART VI

*Two Roads Less Traveled ...
Frequenting Thrift Stores &
Flea Markets*

"When a man is wealthy, he may wear an old cloth."

- ASHANTI

CHAPTER 15

SHAMELESS SHOPPING IN STUFFY STORES
Doing The Second-Hand Shuffle

As I look back over my first acquaintance with thrift (or second hand) stores it is surprising that it would be included as a chapter in this book. My initial experiences were rather unique and comical. You see, my husband, Wendell, grew up knowledgeable about second-hand stores from an aunt who is still a frequent thrift store shopper. Once during our dating relationship, Wendell needed an outfit to attend a social event and was low on cash. He suggested we search out a few thrift stores. Frankly, I had negative opinions about shopping in such places and was embarrassed to go along. When we arrived at the store, I simply couldn't go in. I sat in the car while Wendell shopped. I honestly felt that second-hand stores were exclusively for poor people. At this point in my life, I didn't realize that I was poor too! Nonetheless, he continued to shop at these stores, always encouraging me to come along. One day, I finally did. To my chagrin, it was a fun and exciting adventure. I was hooked! Now, I drop by my favorite thrift store at least three times a week just to cruise the aisles. I believe my car knows the way.

Over the years, I have amassed quite a collection of antiques, rare items and general merchandise to fill my home. Included in this chapter are photos of items my husband and I have acquired. You'll see all kinds of things, from antique Oriental rugs and fine art paintings to a camel leather sofa and beautiful mink coat—all from our local thrift store.

Finding Thrift Stores

Thrift stores are generally found all over the country. Names of common stores include Goodwill and Salvation Army. In addition to these national stores, there are a host of local ones in most cities. These stores are known by a variety of names and frequently include the word "thrift" or "outlet." These second-hand stores are established as non-profit organizations that contribute to social cause such as preventing spousal abuse, child abuse, and homelessness. Therefore, items are widely donated in public support. Not only do individuals donate unwanted items but so do businesses, major department stores, and libraries. National department stores, like TJ Maxx, Macy's and Wal-Mart, consistently donate merchandise at the end of their fiscal year or near tax time for a write-off.

Many of these major stores donate merchandise that is out of season, returned or irregular on a continual basis. Let's not also forget that many families unknowingly donate items, which are of excellent value. Others dump leftover items from garage sales or occasionally toss older items to make room for new things. Considering the possible merchandise that could end up at these stores, it would behoove you to stop and shop! But, before rushing down to the nearest store, there are a few techniques you should master that will make your shopping experience rewarding and memorable.

Technique #1 – Do Your Retail Research. Do your 'retail research' prior to going to a thrift store. Begin by studying various apparels and accessories in retail stores and specialty shops. On your window shopping trips, examine name brands, manufacturing techniques and the overall quality of these items. Be sure to familiarize yourself with the wide range of designers who create fine clothing. When antiquing, visit antique stores to reacquaint yourself with fine antique pieces. For furniture, go to upscale furniture stores and inspect their designs, styles, colors, fabrics, textures and hardware. Also, check out rug stores to inspect handmade oriental rugs and pay close attention to the knotting. Oriental rugs should be tightly woven and without holes. Review and examine everything! The objective is to create an educated, mental profile of fine things. This information will prove invaluable when you cruise the thrift stores.

Antique handmade Chinese oriental rug, purchased for $40, value $600 - $750. Photo: Leon Stoudemire

Technique # 2: Decide When To Go. Trying to decide when to shop is probably hard unless, of course, you talk with an employee or another frequent shopper and ask for the "best times." Stores will have drop off bins and trucks that pickup merchandise from homes all over the city. If you maintain good relations with the clerk behind the counter and other store personnel, they will tell you when the trucks go into certain neighborhoods for pickup. Generally, it only takes one day to replenish and restock dwindling merchandise. So, it is a good idea to visit a

Ranch mink coat, purchased for $150, worth $1100 - $1500.

store the same evening of a 'pick-up day' or early the following morning. Thrift store workers will let you know the 'inside scoop' once friendly rapport is established. They will inform you of rare and unique items (in the back), just waiting to be put out later. Never act grumpy in these stores. Treat the employees with respect and you'll be surprised how far a smile will take you! Otherwise check all of the stores in your area frequently. Try different times of the day. Start with early mornings, and rotate to evenings and weekends. If your schedule permits, checkout the merchandise at least once a week.

Technique #3 - Know What To Look For. Thrift stores are loaded with hidden treasures. You will be surprised at the bargains that you will find. These stores receive donations of essentially any and everything. Always seek quality or interesting items that have a reasonable amount of value or worth. It does not make good economic sense to purchase items that provide no aesthetic, intrinsic or functional value just because of the nominal price. Just because it's cheap, doesn't mean it's good! So, be discriminating about your purchases.

Furniture, clothing, jewelry, linens, appliance, makeup, antiques, and collectibles find there way inside the walls of thrift stores. Look for all of the items you would look for at malls, specialty shops or department stores. Here are a few items to keep your eyes open for:

Linens - Try to find sets quality spreads, embroidered pieces, down comforters, down pillows, handmade crochet, handmade knitting, tablecloths, coverlets, and 100% cotton sheets.

Furniture – Furniture made of solid wood is the best anyone can hope for, since a lot of the pieces made today are made of particle board. Solid wood finds are very desirable and antique furniture is always a tremendous steal!

Books and Magazine – Libraries, colleges, businesses and individuals

Japanese porcelain dresser set, purchased for $5, worth $45.

Oil painting on canvas of young ladies, purchased for $20, worth $275.

donate thousands of books to thrift stores. Adult and children's books are sold from $.25 cents and up. Both rare autographed books and old leather bound books are occasionally available. Current and back issues of magazines are also plentiful for just a few cents.

Mirrors and Art - An array of paintings and mirrors are available at these stores. Expensive charcoal and line drawings, as well as, oil transfers and lithographs have been found. Beveled mirrors with unique carvings are excellent buys. Rare finds include a JFK painting with his original signature on the back and an autographed book by Ernest Hemingway.

Technique #4 – Know How To Shop. One must be a smart shopper to derive great finds. A few helpful hints are in order here. Remember, your 'retail research.' On leisure days, visit different department and specialty stores. Look at cheap vs. expensive items and make a mental comparison. With clothing look at beautiful fabrics. Touch them, train your eyes to recognize them without depending on labels. Frequently, labels are removed from clothing in thrift stores. So, you should learn the classic cuts, styles, and textures of clothing. Once you get accustomed to seeing fine things, it will be easier to recognize them in those "stuffy thrift stores." There are tons of excellent designers from other countries, who are not well known to Americans by labels. Yet, the quality of their merchandise is superb. With frequent visits and much retail training, quality will soon call out to you in the thrift store.

People often ask me, "How do you find the best clothing without looking through the entire rack?" The answer is simple. I look for colors, fabrics and cuts before ever thumbing through racks. This same technique can be applied to searches for shoes, handbags, linens and jewelry. Always look for the unique and extraordinary. In general, people always like something a little different from everyone else.

Technique #5 – Be Aware and Alert. Be aware that your thrift store "finds" will bring envious glances to your shopping cart, so do not leave it unattended. It is not uncommon for a fellow shopper to snatch your goods, right from under your nose!

When looking for antiques and collectibles, invest in a general price guide such as, Schroeder's, or Warman's. These guides have a general listing on a wide variety of items. Included will be a brief description of price and circa (or date). Try to become familiar with the various categories of antiques and collectibles listed in the guides. Having read and studied, items of value will become more recognizable. You may not be looking for a specific item when suddenly something wonderful appears. If it is a popular piece, you will not be the only one to recognize it. Here again, dealers and collectors routinely visit these stores and have developed keen buying sense over the years. If you want it, grab it! Believe me, it will not be there the next time you shop.

English pitcher and bowl set, early 1900s, purchased for $25, worth $150 - $200

Technique #6 – Exchanges and Returns. Most stores will only allow the exchange of merchandise for an in-store credit. Refunds are not normally given. There is no warranty on general merchandise. On the other hand, electrical items carry a thirty day warranty, but the price tag must be attached with an accompanying receipt.

Some stores have dressing rooms and will allow you to try on clothing items. Exchanges on clothing may also be granted, but the same rules apply (price tags attached and receipt in hand). Since refunds are scarce, be reasonably sure of what you want and make *all* selections carefully.

Technique #7 - Wait for the Markdowns. Stores are constantly receiving and pricing new merchandise, so the quick movement of existing items is important. To encourage sales, markdowns on merchandise are done on a week to week basis. A markdown can reflect as much as one-half off. Each week subsequent markdowns are made. For example, an item may start at $9.98 its first week on the racks. The following week the item will be marked down by fifty-percent to $4.99. Each week the item will decrease by half price until it is sold.

"Buyer beware" still applies here. There has been an enormous influx of shoppers to these stores within the last few years. Store personnel have become more aware of the value of items and are pricing accordingly. However, most thrift stores still boast 90% off the retail price.

Technique #8 - To Buy or Not To Buy? That Is The Question! Just as thrift stores can be a fun and economical way to shop, they can also be over-priced. These

Chaps camel leather sofa, purchased for $200, value $1500 - $3000
Photo by Leon Stoudemire.

stores learn exactly how to price their goods from the consumer. When a clerk tags a high price on a thrift store item and you buy it *pronto*, similiar items will remain high until they are ready for markdown. When finding a good buy on something, do not boast of it's value to store employees or openly talk about "deals" where you can be heard. Inevitably, someone will inform the store management. The next time you shop, similar items will be higher priced.

Unless an item is considerably cheaper (or it is an antique or collectible) buy it at another store. If Wal-Mart or Kmart can sell you an identical or similar item for the same amount, it is better to purchase your item there. After all, you may easily return or exchange merchandise in these stores without a problem.

Thrift stores are rapidly becoming the shopping mecca of our nation. Once you get over the shame and realize the savings like I did, thrift stores can be very rewarding places to shop. This chapter has showcased great thrift store finds. As you can see for yourself, these second-hand shopping outlets are exciting and lucrative. You can find *anything* you need or desire within these walls!

This charcoal drawing on canvas of Booker T. Washington was initially priced at $129.99 and after subsequent markdowns was purchased for $35, valued $375.

Dirt [land] is much more valuable than diamond rings.
EARTHA KITT, C.1985

CHAPTER 16

WHEELING & DEALING AT THE FLEA MARKET
Learning To Bargain, Barter and Negotiate

The flea market concept has been around for a long time. The Greeks termed their trade day's "agora." This provided a place for common merchants to sell their goods. The Romans also followed this same general practice. The "forum" was the name assigned to their central marketplace.

Today, flea markets are sometimes referred to as swap-meets or trade days. They are a great place to find unusual bargains. Flea markets are also experiencing a recent revival. Both shoppers and dealers seem to frequent these markets on a regular basis. As the saying goes, "one man's junk, is another man's jewel."

The flea market grounds are usually owned by a local business enterprise and strategically located in a large vacant space. Indoor and outdoor booths are rented to individual vendors for a small fee. These vendors stock and sell a variety of merchandise from new and discounted merchandise to antiques and collectibles. Used (or second-hand) merchandise is also sold. Market days are regularly scheduled and may be daily, weekly, or monthly. Overall, flea market prices are generally lower than retail costs.

In addition to finding general merchandise for sale, fresh fruit and garden vegetables are also available. If you are a hungry shopper, there are plenty of vendors selling popcorn, hot dogs, specialty sandwiches, funnel cakes, and candy apples. Fill up on these goodies as you stroll through the booths in search of new finds or historical riches.

Types of Merchandise

The flea market offers a board spectrum of merchandise. Art, crafts, electronic gadgets, tires, and toiletries can easily be found at the market. Old household goods, used furniture, and the remains of estate (or garage) sales are often brought to market too. So, expect to see all types of merchandise, from the fuzzy and electronic to the rare and handmade.

Most flea markets regulate the type of merchandise that can be sold on the grounds. Pornography, harmful weapons, liquor, stolen goods, illicit drugs, and any other questionable merchandise are generally not allowed. Material that is culturally insensitive or perceived as discriminatory may also be prohibited.

The sale of animals including dogs, cats, rabbits may be restricted to certain areas of the market. The sale of food is restricted as well. Certain types of food may require additional licenses from the local health department. Different states have different regulations depending on type and size of the vendor's operation.

Market Rules Of Order

Other than those restrictions cited above, management bears no warranty, or liability for merchandise. It is customarily sold "as is, where is". Once purchased, items become the responsibility of the buyer. The individual vendor decides whether concessions will be made for damage or theft of property. The vendor also establishes his or her own exchange policies.

All vendors assume full responsibility for all business licenses and necessary taxes that may be due with regard to the sale of merchandise. Terms and conditions of sale (whether cash, check, or credit cards) are left entirely up to the vendor. At some flea markets, the barter system is still alive and well, allowing vendors and buyers to trade merchandise. Bartering is an excellent way to exchange goods.

Overall, management reserves the right to limit the

number of vendors selling similar merchandise. This is done to prevent over-saturation and undue competition.

Buying & Negotiating In The Marketplace

Make all selections at the flea market very carefully. I can't over emphasize this because refunds and exchanges are not common place. When shopping for a particular item, be sure to check out comparative prices and quality. If you are looking for antiques and collectibles, remember to use price guide and reference books to provide the best direction. Though the flea market normally provides a great place to shop, there may be a few vendors waiting to take advantage of the innocent and unknowledgeable. So, be prepared, because there are always fast and smooth talkers to confront.

As with auctions and estate sales, many avid flea market goers prefer to arrive early. This initial time will give you an opportunity to check over the entire grounds, while deciding which booths to visit first. The early bird *really* does get the goods! You will also get an overall idea of price structures set by different vendors. The ones with the best merchandise and prices usually sale out first. Many vendors only bring a test run (or small sample) of merchandise so their quantity may be limited. If you are looking for a antique piece or rare collectible, the vendor may only have one for sale. If you want it, there's a great chance that someone else does too! Being early also has another advantage, dealers will often use this time to shop around with each other and may be more negotiable with prices. On the other hand, staying late can bring good deals and bargains too! The dealer may be willing to part with an item at your price. If you cannot stay all day, try to return just before closing to do some final negotiating. If you feel comfortable with a discounted price, then go ahead and make a purchase--especially if there are limited quantities. However, if an item is still over-priced, then continue your negotiations. Always act as though you can "take it or leave it." Do not appear anxious about a find. Be knowledgeable, articulate, and never let them see you sweat! Once the vendor knows you really want an item, he may attempt to "play hard ball." Stay relaxed! Dealers who have been around the block will sense your "gotta have it" posture and the price will remain unchanged.

Be keenly aware of "value" at all times. Such knowledge will alert you instantly if an item is overpriced. A sharp mind will prevent heartaches later on. Look for quality when selecting merchandise at the market, just as you would anywhere else. Try to develop a rapport with vendors. If you seek a specialty item that the vendor doesn't have, he or she may have friends who do. Sometimes they will locate merchandise for you and keep you in mind for similar items. Building relationships with dealers and vendors will also give you an opportunity to learn about other flea markets or outlets to shop. People tend to be more accommodating with people they like. So, rely on your instincts and be sure to have fun!

Selling Your Wares At Market

Selling at the flea market is probably the most economical way to sale an item. Booths can be rented cheaply on a daily, weekly, or monthly basis. Items can be easily loaded up and brought to an open market with high people volume. But, before you do, make sure you consider the following:

- **Licenses:** Purchase necessary business licenses if you plan to sell on a routine basis. Check out rules regarding one time set up and ongoing sales. Local revenue and taxation departments should be able to answer your questions.
- **Taxes:** Be sure to check your local Department of Revenue regarding tax liability. Some agencies may allow a one-time sale without taxation liability with a business license. For the frequent vendor, be sure to keep up with necessary bookkeeping.
- **Food Sales:** If you want to sell food items, it is best to check with management about applicable permits and licenses.
- **Terms and Conditions of Sale:** Before your first sale, decide whether you will accept personal checks. Most vendors prefer cash. When volume becomes constant and predictable, the acceptance of most major credit cards may be an option.
- **Presentation of Merchandise**: Make sure your booth is neat and organized. This is an essential part of successful sales. All merchandise should be visibly

displayed so bring a colorful table covering to make it more attractive. Buy a large bag of penny candy to place on the table and charge at least a nickel for each piece. At the end of the day, you will have paid for the booth even if you don't sell anything.

- **Price of Merchandise**: Have your merchandise priced so that there is room to bargain. Be mindful of people who openly find flaws in the merchandise. They use this as a tactic and often are good potential buyers.
- **Money Exchange & Safety:** Make sure you have at least one hundred dollars in change to start the day. A fanny pack or some other small attachable purse is best for keeping and exchanging money. Using boxes, purses, or large bags to hold money is generally not a good idea. Hidden or small storage spaces seem to attract the least amount of attention and decrease the chance of theft and robbery. Stay safe!
- **A Family Affair:** Involving your children in the flea market business can be a great way to spend quality time together, while teaching them the importance of customer service, accounting, sales and marketing. Or if they have items they would like to sale to make their own money, having a 'joint venture' could be a real family affair!

PART VII

A Final Hints & Tips For The Savvy Shopper & Collector

We are a wave of fine, impeccably dressed sameness.
RACHEL BROWN, IN *"WINDOW ON THE PARK,"*
CITY ARTS QUARTERLY, FALL-WINTER 1987

CHAPTER 17

A SAVVY SHOPPING & COLLECTING SUMMARY
A Few Things To Keep In Mind

When shopping for antiques, collectibles or general merchandise, you should consider the non-traditional shopping arena of an auction, estate sale, thrift store or flea market. Regardless of the outlet you choose, there are a few basic hints and tips that you should keep in mind.

Do your Homework
When shopping, try to know a little about everything. Read journals, trade magazines, shop department stores and become familiar with the going price of items. Be sure to pick up price guides like Schroeder's Antique Price Guide 1997 (Collection Books) and Warman's Americana & Collectibles—7th Edition (Krause Publications).

Purchase Tools To Assist in Your Research
Pick up a jewelry loupe. They are sold at bookstores, in the stamp collecting sections at your local jewelry store or at general supply outlets. A black light is also needed to detect cracks and breaks in porcelain.

Learn Pertinent Marks and Signs
Learn about appropriate markings on precious metals.

For example, sterling silver which is 925 parts of 1000 will be marked 925, STG, silver or sterling. This means that the silver piece is 925 parts of silver (or 925 out of a 1000). Gold will be indicated by the karat. The markings are 9K, 10K, 14K, 15K, 18K, 22K and 24K. If the markings are 9K or 15K, they represent older pieces.

Be able to Perform Basic Authenticity Tests
If you need to know whether a set of pearls is real, perform the "grainy rub test" across your teeth or bite down on them. If they are gritty, the pearls are genuine. If smooth, they are probably fake.

Learn a few basic things about fabric content and blends
Read the label to help you determine fabric content and blends, as well as, quality and durability. Choose fabrics with 100% cotton versus 50% cotton and 50% polyester blend. When 100% cotton is used — sheets, sweaters, or knit items will feel softer, last longer and look better than cotton and polyester blends. This knowledge will help you when shopping thrift stores and flea markets. Recognize quality based on fabric not labels.

Sleep Like A King and Queen!
Shop for linens with rich dyes and 100% cotton content. Older sheets may be found at auctions and estate sales. While newer sheets, similar in quality, may be purchased at your finer departments stores or closeout stores like Tuesday Morning or TJ Maxx. You should look for Egyptian or Supima cotton sheets with thread counts ranging from 250 to 750. The higher the thread count, the finer the texture and the softer the feel. We all need our royal beauty rest!

Invest In Quality Quilts!
When out shopping, be sure to look at those wonderful quilt, which keeps us so warm. Not to mention the element of pride and the time that our foremothers invested in this historical art form. These women worked diligently with their hands to provide generations with a piece of themselves through quilting. When trying to choose from various quilts, look for flowing patterns and

intricate design. When trying to determine the skills of quilters, take out a ruler and count the number of stitches per inch in a section of quilt. Once you have a count, multiply by two. Twenty stitches or more to the inch are considered crafts of superior skill.

Can you imagine the stories they told while making these? Some of our ancestors went blind on these quilts, in an attempt to pass on an article that would provide personal warmth and a family heirloom for generations.

Select Fine Quality Shoes
Quality shoes will have leather soles. A lot of fine leather shoes are made in Italy and Spain. Look for these international cities on shoe bottoms. Always buy leather, it is beautiful and durable.

Look for Uniqueness
Dare to be different and unique in your selections.
Glance through magazines such as *Architectural Digest, Elle, Essence,* and *The Robb Report*, which is distributed internationally "for the affluent lifestyle". Their mailing address is: Robb Report Subscription Department, Post Office Box 567, Mount Morris, IL 61054-8150. These publications cater to an upscale audience. Their visual presentation will increase your sharpness. Also, visit museums, antiques shops, and major department stores to learn how to train your eye to look for uniqueness.

Limit your Boasting
When you've made an exceptional find at a thrift store—try to hold your tongue, especially while still on the store premises. Keep your excellent finds to yourself, until you are alone with friends and family. Boasting will *only* drive prices up.

Don't Casually Throw Things Away
Check out the items in your possession thoroughly. Call a professional auctioneer or appraiser who will.be able to assist you with value.

Be open minded about where you shop
Shop in unusual places and attend all kinds of sales. Avoid assumptions and narrow-minded thinking. I almost missed some fabulous estate sale items, because I

thought the house with the over-grown grass couldn't possibly have any thing of value inside. Having convinced myself to go in, I was quietly embarrassed that everything was out of my price range! I learned a valuable lesson about shopping that day!

Take Good Care Of Older Linens
Here are a few helpful techniques to address the issues of stains, storage and general cleaning with older linens:

Stain Removal: Stains can be removed from most white pieces by mixing 1 tsp. sodium perborate with 1 gallon of water, then soaking for several hours. This solution will remove most stains and produce beautiful linen for you to display.

Storage: When storing large spreads and quilts, try to roll and not fold them. Folding develops creases, weakens the fibers and causes tears in the fabric. Proper storing is extremely important to preserving your linens.

General Cleaning: The use of starches and other chemicals over a period of time will also weaken fabrics. Do not use harsh detergents such as, bleach (Clorox). Ivory Snow flakes and Wiz will gently clean your linens without harming them.

Have A Lotta Fun!
Antiquing, auctioning, shopping, bartering and negotiating are excellent ways to have fun with family and friends. Set aside a whole day to go on "a treasure hunt" and see what kind of things each person can find. Be sure to start out with a small list of items you're looking for...you'll be thrilled at what you find at the end of the day.

PART VIII

Moving Forward On A Lighted Path

> *"Those from among you will rebuild the ancient ruins; you will raise up the age-old foundations; and you will be called the repairer of the breach. The restorer of streets in which to dwell."*
>
> ISAIAH 58:13-15

CHAPTER 18

AFTERWORD: A PRACTICAL MANDATE FOR FAMILIES
Lighting Up the Path...Passing On the Riches

Many African-American families have lost their internal compass. They have drifted off course and forsaken the simple traditions of transferring legacy, establishing keepsakes and maintaining heritage. The timeless truths of our foreparents have become like ancient ruins and the age-old foundations they reared us on have been broken down.

From Darkness To Light is our "clarion call" across the land. It is a unique guide with a spiritual message seeking to undergird a practical mandate: *To pass on articles of value and words of wisdom to every generation.*

This modern guide is an ageless gift for every family that desires to recapture historical riches. As we approach the 21st century, the struggles and accomplishments of this era will need to be preserved for posterity, and communicated through future generations.

Our mandate to families goes beyond class, status, educational attainment and income. From the projects to the penthouse, each of us must commit to equip our children with a heritage that will empower them to compete and achieve in the global market. Beyond the latest toys, sneakers, and video games; we must provide historical, spiritual and cultural *connections* for our children that are strong and unfading.

In order to accomplish this goal, we should provide our children with a few principles that have historically served the African-American family. These principles enables us to revisit, reclaim, restore and rebuild in modern times. In this light, we seek to inspire African-American families to:

Revisit Our Historic Contributions: Applaud and appreciate the rich contributions that African-American artisans have made to America. Read and talk about these "keepers of the culture" with your children. Plan visits to libraries, museums and cities where their works are on display. Acquire the creations of new artists who have an assortment of art, sculpture, pottery, porcelain and apparel for varying styles and tastes.

Read more African-American biographies and subscribe to magazines that reflect black history and heritage. Two excellent magazines to begin with are:

about...time Magazine
283 Genesee Street
Rochester, NY 14611
716-235-7150

American Legacy Magazine
Post Office Box 5440
Harlan, IA 51593-2940
1-800-454-4997

Confront the negative realities and positive developments we have experienced throughout our sojourn in this country. Collect black memorabilia. Accessorize with quilts and decorate with African motifs.

Reclaim Our Ancestral Heritage: We must declare with pride that we are "Africa's New World Children." Our ancestral lineage flows back to the continent of Africa with its many tribes and throughout the Diaspora. We have a derivation, a place or origin, a homeland! We are African-Americans with roots that stretch across the Atlantic Ocean and down into the Caribbean and around the Seven Seas. These "connections" can never be disclaimed or ignored. Our internal make-up and external design collectively sings a melody of African styles and influences. This must be reclaimed and forever settled in our hearts.

Restore Cross-Generational Family Time: We should plan big, annual, family reunions, as well as, small, weekly, Get-Togethers that include *everyone,* from our youngsters to our elders. Historically, we have been blessed by cross-generational family systems where every member was esteemed, respected and supported—no matter their "stage" in life. Generational gaps are a hindrance to any goals for family unity and closeness.

Therefore, we should commit to resurrect family dinners and establish weekly 'talk-times' where individual accomplishments and family stories can be openly shared. Our lives must be emptied of "me, myself and I" or "us four and no more!" We are enriched and enlarged through self-sacrifice and connectedness to others. It would be exciting to revive the Sunday-Soon-As-Church-Is-Over-Dinner or Friday-Night-Fish Fry, allowing our homes to resonate with the sounds of extended family, close friends and others who would benefit from the atmosphere. During the holiday season, we can unite with other families to celebrate Christmas and Kwanzaa as a lasting tradition of spiritual and cultural heritage.

Our homes must become 'community centers,' especially for our teens; who complain of social boredom and display mental idleness. As African-Americans, in particular, we have become too isolated and estranged from one another — even though we live within the same four walls. Everyone moves to the beat of a different drummer and there is only a faint melody between us. This cannot be! As parents, we will have to work a few hours less and miss a few more networking opportunities to show this generation how to have good, clean, contagious FUN!

- **It will take playing together!** When was the last time your family played kick ball, challenged one another in your favorite board games or entertained each other with a lively display of (hip-hop) charades?
- **It will take dining together!** Consider hosting an elegant evening of fine dining for your children and several of their friends - *blacktie!* Here's your chance to use the antique finds, collectible porcelain and beautiful cut glass you have acquired. It will be a festive and unforgettable evening for everyone.
- **It will take performing together!** I vividly recall Uncle Tom training my cousins and me to sing *a* flawless rendition of *"To Dream The Impossible*

Dream." Or having to show off my new dress, while reciting my Easter speech for relatives who came to partake of the traditional 'baked ham with all the trimmings' on Easter Sunday. Today, our house is filled with verbal presentations from skits and musical recitals to Scripture memory and dramatic readings. The key is to become a consummate performer! Children, young and old, love to have adults entertain them. Before you know it, you'll be an audience of one and they'll be reciting Frederick Douglas or Sojourner Truth and doing choreographed dance movements across the living room floor.

- ***It will take collecting together!*** Everyone has a special interest; and one that is shared with others becomes even more special. Have each child identify one subject area that they "just love." It could be a collection of stamps, dolls or baseball cards! As birthdays and other important days come around, it won't be hard to choose special gifts for one another. The goal is to create the lasting discipline and appreciation in your children for rare, valuable items that can be treasured throughout their lifetime and beyond!

Rebuild Insulated Communities: Strong families make strong communities. As part of our recapturing historical riches, we must recreate caring communities where every member, from the eldest to the youngest, is supported. More than anything, African-American communities have lost a sense of "connectedness." We should know our neighbors intimately, spend time with extended family members, volunteer in local schools and give liberally to those less fortunate. In this way, we can create village-like communities that are safe and insulated again.

From the family unit, we are to emerge empowered to take a bold stand in the world. Schools facilitate and churches undergird – but the legacy of "passing on" articles of wealth and words of wisdom must begin and be maintained by the family system. Below are four practical mandates that can enrich the lives of families and keep an eternal flame burning in the hearts of each member.

Special Keepsakes
Every family should possess special keepsakes that can

be cherished and adored by its members throughout time. Keepsakes are characterized as items resurrected from Grandmother's attic, collectibles purchased at an estate sale or whatnots with strong sentimental value. These special pieces can be "passed on" to a chosen offspring who will commit to maintain the item's history during their lifetime and make plans for its preservation once they are gone.

Oral Traditions

Families must revive oral traditions through the sharing of significant stories! Older members, in particular, must verbally reenact the events of people, places and possessions that make the family unique. Children must be able to "hear, touch, see and feel" their connection to others who have gone on before them. Oral traditions will create family bridges upon which family offspring can pass over. Oral traditions will also develop "gate keepers," who will watch and guard over the intangible riches that never loose their value.

It was the single element of "oral traditions" that helped the late Alex Hailey, trace his *Roots* and pass on to each of us 'the saga of an American family.' When Hailey was a boy, his grandmother used to tell him stories about their family. These "stories went back to *her* grandparents, their grandparents and down through the generations all the way to a man called 'the African.'" Her narrative provided an adult Hailey with an inner desire to document and authenticate the oral tradition. *Roots* is a rich and lasting legacy that spans two continents and two centuries! It reveals the amazing power of simple, passionate stories to keep the family flame burning throughout time. Oral traditions are endearing and profitable.

Spiritual Heritage

Along with special keepsakes and oral traditions, families must exercise and communicate a spiritual heritage to its members. Young children and growing teens must have a clear and realistic understanding of faith. "Why do we believe this?" "Why is this so important?" "How come we celebrate this way?" These are general questions that should be acknowledged with simple and heart-felt responses. Such questions become more complex as our children mature and encounter hardships in the world.

When God delivered the Israel people out of Egyptian slavery, Moses admonished the parents to teach the Laws and Commandments of God to their children. "Only give heed to yourself and keep your soul diligently, lest you forget the things which your eyes have seen, and lest they depart from your heart all the days of your life; but make them known to your sons and your grandsons." (Deuteronomy 4:9)

"Teach them (the Laws and Commandments) diligently," Moses exhorted Israel. "Talk of them when you walk by the way and when you lie down and when you rise up." It was important that God was not just 'the man upstairs' or some ethereal Sovereign disconnected from their lives. His words and desires were not a Sunday morning only event. Jehovah God along with His Laws and Commandments were to be clearly observed and acknowledged each and everyday of their lives.

In a final admonition, Moses spoke of the importance of knowing God intimately, seeing His Word and doing His Will so that His Laws and Commands would not be violated or forgotten, especially by the children. "And you shall write them on the door posts of your house and on your gates." In other words, it was to be very, very clear what the family believed! It was important that God's Word was obeyed first inside the home, then outwardly for others to see. Anyone playing with their children, visiting their home, talking with them in their fields or walking by their "gate" should have been able to clearly realize the faith and beliefs of the nation of Israel.

Likewise, King David, strongly exhorted the Israelites in Psalms 78 saying,

> "Listen, O my people, to my instruction; Incline your ears to the words of my mouth. I will open my mouth in a parable; I will utter dark sayings of old, which we have heard and known, and our fathers have told us. We will not conceal them for their children, but tell to the generation to come the praises of the Lord, and His strength and His wonderful works that He has done."

King David goes on to remind the Israelites of how God gave them a testimony, appointed just laws to govern them and commanded them as parents (and especially fathers) to keep the laws and commands of God and to:

> "Teach them to their children, that the generation to come might know, even the children yet to be born, that they may arise and tell them to their children, that they should put their confidence in God and not forget the works of God, but keep His commandments."

Too often our children grow-up spiritually malnourished with small faith and no anchor to hold them through the inevitable storms of life. How desperately they need a clear understanding of the Invisible, All Powerful One!

When Kizzy was born to Kunta Kinte in Alex Haley's *Roots,* he took his day-old infant under the midnight sky and lifted her up to the heavens. In his native Mandinka tongue, he spoke to her this spiritual truth: *"Behold, the only thing greater than yourself!"* How much our modern children need a well-communicated, spiritual heritage. They must encounter the great "I Am" and become personally acquainted with "the God of our weary years, the God of our silent tears." The One who has blessed and kept the family through many toils and snares.

Material Inheritance

After reading *From Darkness To Light,* you should be filled with creative ways to acquire valuable antiques, collectibles and other personal property that can be passed down from generation to generation. Many will already have heirlooms or rare items within the family. Others will have to search around for important pieces. Whatever, you have to do, the mandate is clear: *To leave an inheritance to your children and your children's children!*

Many African-American families, however, fail to designate a *specific child* for a *particular possession or aspect* of the family inheritance. Too, often we generally scribble "share and share alike" in a parting note. Or leave personal property like a home, automobile or dining room set in a formal will indicating that such items are "to be split six ways." This is an unfortunate request which causes family feuds and distressful hardships among grieving siblings and other family members.

A much wiser way to impart material inheritance, is through a legal document which chronicles the history of a specific possession, clearly identifies a family steward and gives ample reasons why that person has been chosen. Decisions should be made based on years of observation, fair assessments of character, a working knowledge of personal interests and much prayer. Below is a fictional example of how material inheritance can be imparted from one generation to another:

> *"My daughter, Mary Ann Brown Hall will receive the Steinway piano, circa 1887, that has been in the Brown family for five generations. The piano was purchased by Anna Mae Brown Williams in 1910 for $28. She served as a dedicated music teacher and educator at the Hillside Methodist Church in West Alton until her death in 1953. On August 15, 1990, the Steinway piano was appraised by Pettyway Appraisals for $21,000. Documentation is enclosed. A monetary gift of $5,000 is attached herewith to be used to restore the piano's physical beauty and to make any minor repairs. Mary Ann has been chosen as the family steward over this musical inheritance because of her intense love for music, faithfulness to keep the 'beat' at family gatherings and overall accomplishments in music theory and appreciation at Lowell High School. Mary Ann, I pray that you will enjoy this 'historic treasure' for many years and at the end of your days "pass it on" to a deserving family member of your choosing. May the Lord use this piano as a reminder of your musical calling and responsibility to keep the melody of this family vibrant and alive. With Love and Appreciation, Mom."*

In order to provide your offspring with an appropriate inheritance that they will cherish and preserve, you should ask yourself questions like:

- "Who has demonstrated the best financial responsibility in this family?
- Which of the children will cherish these old quilts and tell their stories?
- Who will be able to uproot and be responsible for the upkeep and maintenance of the family home?
- Does my grandchild have an interest in antique cars or is he into new modern vehicles?
- Would this antique bedroom suite that has been used by several generations be appreciated more by my granddaughter or niece?
- Which of the children would benefit from these stocks and bonds and continue to invest wisely in them?
- Of my three sons, who can best serve as a wise and fair executor of this estate?

This kind of thought-provoking analysis will benefit the entire family. Your children will know that you have given serious considerations to the family "riches." Disagreements and disappointments may still prevail, but your wishes will be clearly communicated. Ultimately, they will respect your desires and see your wisdom..

By now the light should be bright and brilliant in your heart. You have journeyed across time and territory in an effort to recapture historical riches. We have highlighted the life and work of four African-American artisans; unveiled the world of auctions and estate sales; defined the period and styles of antiques; highlighted the value of black and other collectibles; reviewed thrift stores and flea markets; and offered you a few hints and tips on becoming a savvy shopper and collector.

As a family, we have been challenged to preserve special keepsakes, maintain oral traditions of storytelling, communicate a spiritual heritage and wisely choose an appropriate steward for every aspect of our material inheritance. All of this information has been packaged for one single purpose: *To inspire each one of us to pass on something of value to our offspring.*

May you enjoy your new knowledge and use it boldly! "Arise and shine for the light has come!"

PART IX

The Appendix...
Essentials For The Journey

African-American Decorative Resources

Antiques

Center for African American Arts
2221 Peachtree Road
Suite D-341
Atlanta, GA 30309
(404) 605-0734
African-American decorative arts and antiques

Findings
246 Race Street
Philadelphia, PA 19106
(215) 923-0988
Antiques, reproductions, and collectibles

Malmaison Antiques
253 E. 74th Street
New York, NY 10021
(212) 288-7569
Egyptian Revival and Empire furniture

Sandra Klim
401 S. Guadeloupe Street
Santa Fe, NM 87501
(505) 986-0340
International antiques, artifacts and textiles

Craftspeople & Artisans

Chris Clark
1420 20th Place Ensley
Birmingham, AL 35218
(205) 785-5457
Quilter and Folk Artist

Sweetgrass Baskets
532 E. Wimbledon Drive
Charleston, SC 29412
(803) 722-4810
Baskets & other decorative arts

Shining Iron - Ogun Productions
Mustafa A., Artist & Blacksmith
1113 7th Avenue W
Birmingham, AL 35204
(205) 786-8830
ornamental wrought iron

Philip Simmons Foundation
P. Simmons, Master Craftsman
91 Anson Street
Post Office Box 21585
Charleston, SC 29413-1585
(803) 723-8018
ornamental wrought iron, decorative arts

Arts and Crafts

Out of Africa
3641 Magazine Street
New Orleans, LA
(504) 945-9115
African arts and crafts

Window to Africa
5210 S. Harper Court
Chicago, IL 60615
(312) 955-7742
Traditional African art, crafts, and fashion

Anne Hooks, Folk Artist
1529 Matt Leonard Drive, SW
Birmingham, AL 35236
(205) 942-0213
Accessory designs, ethnic pottery and African art

Colors of Africa
129 Berkshire Lane
Fort Worth, TX 76134
Antique African trade beads

184   THE APPENDIX: ESSENTIALS FOR THE JOURNEY

CUSTOM FURNITURE
INTERIOR DESIGN

Afuture
241 Avenue of the Americas
New York, NY 10014
(212) 724-7631
Custom furniture design

Alternative Design
334 Barrow Street
Jersey City, NJ 07302
(201) 413-0094
Custom design and interiors

Cheryl Sutton and Associates
130 Morningside Avenue
Gary, IN 46408
(219) 981-3991
National art dealers

Design Glory
Angeline Stallworth
1951 East Bend Circle #N
Birmingham, AL 35215
(205) 856-0976
Interior Designer

TEXTILES

A & J Fabrics
752 S. Fourth Street
Philadelphia, PA 19147
(215) 592-7011
Traditional and African-inspired textiles

Kimberly House Ltd.
120 W. 86th Street
New York, NY 10024
(212) 977-6907
South African textiles

LFS Enterprises
for Wonoo Ventures, Ltd.
1657 The Fairway, Suite 150
Jenkinstown, PA 19056
(215) 782-8489
Traditional Ghanaian Kente cloth, stools

Revman Industries Inc.
1211 Avenue of Americas
New York, NY 10036
(212) 840-7780
Bedding, home textiles

Quilters of the Round Table
5038 Hazel Avenue
Philadelphia, PA 19143
(215) 748-5022
African-American quilt

African-American Educational Mini Directory

Afro-American Historical and Cultural Museum
701 Arch Street
Philadelphia, PA 19106
(215) 574-0380
African-American arts and cultural center

Alit Ash Kebede Fine Art
964 N. LaBrea Avenue
Los Angeles, CA 90038
(213) 874-6269
Fine African and African-American Art

Bethune-Cookman College Carl S. Swisher Library
640 2nd Avenue
Daytona Beach, FL 32015
African-American archives

Black Archives Research Center and Museum
Florida A&M University
Post Box 809
Tallahassee, FL 32307
African-American archives

Bomani Gallery
251 Post Street
San Francisco, CA 94108
(415) 296-8677
International and decorative art

Craft Caravan
63 Greene Street
New York, NY 10012
(212) 431-6669
African-American artifacts

Civil Rights Institute
520 16th Street North
Birmingham, Alabama 35203
(205) 328-9696
Documentation of Civil Rights Movement and International Human Rights archives

Eric Robertson African Arts
36 W. 22nd Street
New York, NY 10010
(212) 675-4045
Traditional African art

Gallery of Art
Morgan State University
Baltimore, MD 21239
African-American art

Indigo Arts
153 N. Third Street
Philadelphia, PA 19106
(215) 922-4041
Ethnographic, folk, and contemporary art

Lithos' Gallery
6301 Bdelmar
St. Louis, MO 63130
(314) 862-0674
Traditional African art and American art

Martin Luther King, Jr. Center for Social Change
503 Auburn Avenue, NE
Atlanta, Georgia 30312
Teaching non-violence and elements of social reform

Moorland-Spingarn Research Center
Howard University
Washington, DC 20059
African-American experience

Museum of African-American History
315 Warren Avenue
Detroit, MI
(313) 494-5800

Museum of Fine Arts, Boston
465 Huntington Avenue
Boston, Massachusetts 02115
(617) 267-9300
Harriet Power's 1898 Quilt

National Afro-American Museum & Cultural Center
1350 Brush Row Road
Wilberforce, OH 45384
(513) 376-4944
African American and African art

North Carolina Museum of Art History
2110 Blue Ridge Road
Raleigh, North Carolina 27607
(919) 839-6262
Thomas Day furniture collection

Philip Simmons Foundation
Post Office 21585
Charleston, SC 29413
(803) 723-8018
Documenting Ornamental Ironwork in Charleston by Master Craftsman, Philip Simmons

Porter Randall Gallery
5624 LaJolla Boulevard
LaJolla, CA 92037
(619) 551-8884
African art

Robbins Center for Cross-Cultural Communication
530 Sixth Street, SE
Washington, DC 20003
African arts and informational center on cross-cultural relationships

Rhode Island Black Heritage Society
1 Hilton Street
Providence, RI 02907
African-American archives

Schomberg Center for Research in Black Culture
New York Library
515 Lenox Avenue
New York, New York 10037
African-American research and culture

Smithsonian Institute
Museum of American History
Division of Textiles
14th & Consitution Avenue, NW
Washington, DC 20560
(205) 357-1889
Harriet Power's 1886 Quilt

Southern Center for Afro-American Architecture
Tuskegee Institute
308 Gregory Street
Tuskegee, AL 36088
archives on architecture

The Charleston Museum
360 Meeting Street
Charleston, SC 29403
(803) 722-2996
Dave The Potter Collection

Antique & Collectibles Publications & Periodicals

Trade Newspapers

The Maine Antique Digest
P.O. Box 1429
Waldboro, ME 04572
1-207-832-4888
Published monthly, at $29 for an annual subscription. Big antique bargain. This publication is read by dealers and collectors around the country. Lots of auction news, with prices. Show notices, display ads and classifieds are also included.

Antiques and the Arts Weekly
Bee Publishing Company
5 Church Hill Road
Newtown, CT 08470
1-203-426-3141
An annual subscription, $38. A weekly publication, similar in format to *The Maine Antique Digest*.

Regional Guides & Newsletters

Antique Almanac
The New York Eye Publishing Co., Inc.
P.O. Box 2400
New York, NY 10021
Ten dollars per year for twelve issues. Small publication covering New York state.

Antique & Collectibles
Box 1565
El Cajon, CA 92022
Features news and articles about California and some about Arizona

Antique Review
12 East Stafford Avenue
Worthington, OH 43085
Features the mid-western states.

The Antique Shopper
37600 Hills Tech Drive
Farmington Hills, MI 48331
Twelve monthly issues for $19. Small mid-western publication with plenty of auction news.

Antique Trader
Post Office Box 1050
Dubuque, IA 52004-1050
A large weekly circulation covering the mid-western states. One-year subscription, $35 for 52 weekly issues.

Antiques Gazette
Post Office Box 305
Hammond, LA 70404
1-504-429-0575
Published monthly, 12 issues for $14. Covers the entire southern region from Florida to Houston.

The Antique Journal
Post Office Box 120
Ware, MA 01082
An excellent publication with lots of illustrations and interesting articles. Covers the entire Northeastern United States. Twelve issues for $12 per year.

The County Register
6055 East Lake Mead Boulevard
#A164
Las Vegas, NV 89115-6909
Published every two months for an annual subscription of $12. Information covers the state of Nevada.

Fence Posts
421 Main Street
Windsor, LA 80550
1-800-275-5646
Published weekly; $27 per year. Features a lot of western and Midwestern farm and ranch auctions.

Flea Market Shoppers Guide
Post Office Box 8
LaHabra, CA 90633-0008
Distributed free at most California flea markets. Write for subscription price and general information.

MassBay Antiques
Community Newspaper Company
2 Washington Street
Post Office Box 192
Ipswich, MA 01938
One-year subscription costs $15. Serving Massachusetts, Rhode Island and Connecticut.

Today's Collector
700 East State Street
Iola, WI 54990-0001
Twelve issues for $17.95. This "glossy newsmagazine" covers the entire United States. An excellent buy for news and resources.

WHERE TO BUY:
CATALOGS & OTHER RESOURCES

Antique Bottle & Glass Magazine
102 Jefferson Street
Post Office Box 180
East Greenville, PA 18041
Published monthly for $3 per copy and $19 annual subscription

Antique Purses Catalog
Bayhouse
Post Office Box 40443
Bay Village, OH 44140
(216) 871-8584
Includes colored photos of bead and enameled mesh purses.

Antique Souvenir Collector's News
Post Office Box 562
Great Barrington, MA 01230

Black Memorabilia Illustrated Sales List
Cookie Jars and Go Withs Illustrated Sales List
Disneyana Illustrated Sales List
Send $2 and LSASE each. Buy, sell and collect.
May-October: R.D. 1, Box 273 SC,
                  Effort, PA 18330
                  (717) 629-6583
Nov.-April: 4195 S. Tamiami Trail, #183SC
                  Venice, FL 34293
                  (941) 497-7149

Cookie Jarrin' With Joyce: The Cookie Jar Newsletter
R.R. 2, Box 504
Walterboro, SC 29488

Depression Glass Daze
Box 57, Otisville, MI 48463
(313) 631-4593
The nation's marketplace for glass, china and pottery.

Hake's Americana & Collectibles
Specializing in character and personality collectibles along with artifacts of popular culture for over 20 years. To receive a catalog for their next 3,000-item mail/phone bid auction, send $3 to
                  Hake's Americana
                  Post Office Box 1444M
                  York, PA 17405

International Perfume and Scent Bottle Collectors Association
Post Office Box 529
Vienna, VA 22183
or Fax (703) 242-1357
Annual Membership: $35
Newsletter published quarterly

Iron Talk
Post Office Box 68
Waelder, TX 78959
Journal of antique pressing irons; News of prices, patents, markets, collectibles, collectors, history, reference, advice and much more; One-year bimonthly subscription: $25 (Texas residents add $1.94 tax)

Kitchen Antiques & Collectibles News
Collectors of Old Kitchen Stuff
4645 Laurel Ridge Drive
Harrisburg, PA 17110
(717) 545-7320
Subscription: $24 per year for 6 issues

Blue Marlin Company
Eric Stuebe, President
San Francisco, CA
(415) 512-0208
Negro Baseball League caps

M&J Enterprises
Mike & Jackie Linley
Rockmart, Georgia
(770) 684-6361
Negro Baseball League caps, apparel and other Black memorabilia

AUCTION SCHOOLS

American Academy of Auctioneers
1222 N. Kenwood
Broken Arrow, OK 74012

Associated Auction School
753 Toni Drive
Hurst, Texas 76054

Florida Auctioneer Academy
1212 East Colonial Drive
Orlando, FL 32803
(305) 896-9797

International School of Auction
Route 5
South Deerfield, MA
(413) 665-2977

Mason City College of Auctioneering
Post Office Box 1463
Mason City, IA 50401

Mendenhall School of Auctioneering
Post Office Box 7344
High Point, NC 27263
(919) 887-1165

Missouri Auction School
1600 Genesee
Kansas City, MO 64102

Nashville Auction School
Post Office Box 190
Lawrenceburg, TN 38464

National Institute of Real Estate Auctioneers
3961 MacArthur Blvd., #212
Newport Beach, CA 92660

World Wide College of Auctioneering
Post Office Box 949
Mason City, IA 50401
(515) 423-5242

Reppert School of Auctioneering
Post Office Box 189
Decatur, IN 46733
(219) 724-3804

STATE AUCTIONEER LICENSING AGENCIES

ALABAMA
State Board of Auctioneers
Post Office Box 56
Montgomery, AL 36101
(334) 263-3407

ALASKA
Division of Occupational Licensing
3601 C Street
Suite #722
Anchorage, AK 99503
(907) 563-2169

ARIZONA
Department of Revenue
License and Registration Section
1600 W. Monroe
Phoenix, AR 85007
(602) 542-2076, ext.50

CALIFORNIA
The California Auctioneer Commission has been discontinued. No license required.

COLORADO
Division of Real Estate
1776 Logan Street
Denver, CO 80203
(303) 894-2166

CONNECTICUT
Connecticut Department of Consumer Protection and Real Estate
165 Capitol Avenue, Room G8
Hartford, CT 06106
(203) 566-5130

DELAWARE
Delaware Division of Revenue
Carvel State Office Building
820 North French Street
Wilmington, DE 198-1

DISTRICT OF COLUMBIA
Department of Consumer and Regulatory Affairs
614 H. Street, N.W.
Washington, D.C. 20001
(202) 727-7100

FLORIDA
Department of Professional Regulation
1940 North Monroe Street
Tallahassee, FL 32399-0762
(904) 488-5189

GEORGIA
Georgia Auctioneers Commission
166 Pryor Street, S.W.
Atlanta, GA 30303
(404) 656-2282

HAWAII
City and County of Honolulu
Department of Finance, Motor Vehicle and Licensing
1455 S. Bretania Street
Honolulu, HI 96814
(808) 973-2810

IDAHO
Real Estate Commission
Statehouse Mail
Boise, ID 83720-6000
(208) 334-3285

ILLINOIS
Office of the Governor
Ronald J. Fagan State Services Representative
Springfield, IL 62706

INDIANA
Indiana Professional Licensing Agency
1021 Indiana Government Center North
100 North Senate Avenue
Indianapolis, IN 46204-2246
(317) 232-2980

IOWA
Department of Agriculture and Land Stewardship
Wallace Building
Des Moines, IA 50319
(515) 281-5322

KANSAS
Office of the Attorney General
Second Floor, Kansas Judicial Center
Topeka, KS 66612-1597
(913) 296-2215

KENTUCKY
Kentucky Board of Auctioneers
9112 Leesgate Road, Suite 5
Louisville, KY 40222
(502) 595-4453

LOUISIANA
Louisiana Auctioneers Licensing Board
8017 Jefferson Highway, Suite B-3
Baton Rouge, LA 70809
(504) 925-3921

State Auctioneer Licensing Agencies

MAINE
Department of Professional & Financial Regulation
State House Station #35
Augusta, ME 04333
(207) 582-8723

MARYLAND
Revenue-generating trader's license required from the local county where auctioneer has place of business. Check with local county licensing agency.

MASSACHUSETTS
Division of Standards
One Ashburton Place
Boston, MA 02108
(617) 727-3480

MICHIGAN
Bureau of Occupation and Profession Regulation
Real Estate Board
Post Office Box 30018
Lansing, MI 48909
(517) 373-0490

MINNESOTA
Application and fees must be made to county auditors throughout state.

MISSISSIPPI
Secretary of State
Post Office Box 136
Jackson, MS 39205
(601) 359-1604

MISSOURI
Auction licenses are issued through the respective county commissions around the state.

MONTANA
Department of Commerce
Business Licensing Specialist
1424 Ninth Avenue
Helena, MT 59620
(406) 444-3923

NEBRASKA
Real Estate Commission
Post Office 94667
Lincoln, NE 68509
(502) 471-2004

NEVADA
Real Estate Division
1665 Hot Springs Road
Las Vegas, NV 89710
(702) 687-4280

NEW HAMPSHIRE
Board of Auctioneers
Secretary of State Office,
State House, Room #204
Concord, NH 0331
(603) 271-3242

NEW JERSEY
The state does not require an auctioneer license. However, auction permits and licenses are under local government control. Each jurisdiction sets its own fees and requirements.

NEW MEXICO
Regulaton and Licensing Department
725 Street Michael's Drive
Santa Fe, NM 87504
(505) 827-7006

NEW YORK STATE
New York State Office of Business Permits & Regulator Assistance
AESOB, 17th Floor
Post Office Box 7027
Albany, NY 12225
(518) 474-8275

NORTH CAROLINA
North Carolina Auctioneer Licensing Board
Suite 306, Haworth Building
3509 Haworth Drive
Raleigh, NC 27609
(919) 733-2182

NORTH DAKOTA
Public Service Commission of North Dakota
Grain Elevator Division
State Capitol
Bismarck, ND 58505
(701) 224-4082

OHIO
Ohio Department of Commerce
Division of Licensing
77 S. High Street, 23rd Floor
Columbus, OH 43266-0546
(614) 466-4130

OKLAHOMA
Governing agencies are established through county treasurers and municipalities.

OREGON
Real Estate Agency
158 12th Street, North East, 2nd Floor
Salem, OR 97310
(503) 378-4170

PENNSYLVANIA
State Board of Auctioneer Examiners
Post Office Box 2649
Harrisburg, PA 17105-2649
(717) 783-3397

RHODE ISLAND
Department of Business Regulation
Division of Licensing and Consumer Protection
233 Richmond Street, Suite #230
Providence, RI 02903-4230
(401) 277-3857

SOUTH CAROLINA
South Carolina Auctioneer's Commission
1200 Main Street, Suite 301
Columbia, SC 29201
(803) 734-1220

SOUTH DAKOTA
Real Estate Commission
Post Office Box 490
Pierre, SD 57501-0490
(605) 773-3600

TENNESSEE
Department of Commerce & Insurance
Auctioneer Commission
500 James Robertson Parkway
Nashville, TN 37243-1152
(615) 741-3236

TEXAS
Texas Department of Licensing & Regulation
Post Office 12157
Austin, TX 78711
(512) 463-3173

UTAH
Department of Commerce
Post Office Box 45802
Salt Lake City, UT 84145-0802
(801) 530-6955

VERMONT
Secretary of State
Office of Regulation
109 State Street
Montpelier, VT 05609-1106
(802) 828-2191

VIRGINIA
Department of Commerce
Auctioneer Section
3600 W. Broad Street
Richmond, VA 23230-4917
(804) 367-8554

WASHINGTON
Auctioneer Section
Post Office Box 9020
Olympia, WA 98507-9020
(206) 586-4575

WEST VIRGINIA
West Virginia Department of Agriculture
Marketing & Development Division
East Wing, State Capitol
Charleston, WV 25305
(304) 348-2210

WISCONSIN
Department of regulation and Licensing
Post Office Box 8935
Madison, WI 53708
(608) 266-5439

WYOMING
Wyoming Attorney General
123 Capitol Building
Cheyenne, WY 82002
(307) 777-7841

GSA Mailing List
Personal Property Division

REGION 1: Connecticut, Maine, Massachusetts, New Hampshire, Rhode Island, Vermont: *John W. McCormack Post Office and Courthouse Boston, MA 02109*

REGION 2: New York, New Jersey, Puerto Rico, Virgin Islands: *26 Federal Plaza, New York, NY 10007*

REGION3: District of Columbia, Delaware, Maryland, Pennsylvania, Virginia, West Virginia: *7th and D Streets SW, Washington, DC 20407*

REGION 4: Alabama, Florida, Georgia, Kentucky, Mississippi, North Carolina, South Carolina, Tennessee: *1776 Peachtree Street, NW Atlanta, GA 30309*

REGION 5: Illinois, Indiana, Michigan, Minnesota, Ohio, Wisconsin: *230 South Dearborn St., Chicago, IL 60604*

REGION 6: Iowa, Kansas, Missouri, Nebraska: *1500 East Bannister Rd., Kansas City, MO 64131*

REGION 7: Arkansas, Louisiana, New Mexico, Oklahoma, Texas: *819 Taylor St. Forth Worth, TX 76102*

REGION 8: Colorado, Montana, North Dakota, South Dakota, Utah, Wyoming: *Denver Federal Center Bldg., 41 Denver, CO 80225*

REGION 9: American Samoa, Arizona, California, Guam, Hawaii, Nevada, the Trust Territory of the Pacific Islands: *525 Market Street, San Francisco, CA 94105*

REGION 10: Alaska, Idaho, Oregon, Washington: *GSA, Auburn, WA 98002*

Department of Defense
Property Disposal Division

REGION 1: DPDR-Columbus, Attn: *DPDR-CMB 3900 E. Broad St., Columbus, OH 43215*

REGION 2: DPDR-MMB *2163 Airways Blvd., Memphis, TN 38114*

REGION 3: DPDR-OMB *500 W. 12th Street Ogden, UT 84401*

REAL ESTATE: *Department of Defense, Surplus Property Sales, Post Office Box 1370, Battle Creek, MI 49016*

BIBLIOGRAPHY

The following books and periodicals were used in our research and writing of this book.

Algotsson, Sharne and Davis, Denys. *The Spirit of African Design*. New York, NY: Clarkson N. Potter, 1996.

Chase, Judith Wragg. *Afro-American Art and Craft*. New York, NY: Van Nostrand Reinhold Company, 1971.

DeForrest, Michael. *How To Buy at Auction*. New York, NY: Simon Schuster, 1972.

Duncan, Alastair. *Art Nouveau and Art Deco Lighting*. New York, NY: Simon and Schuster, 1978.

Durant, Mary. *The American Heritage Guide To Antiques*. Canada: American Heritage Publishing Co., 1970.

Florence, Gene, ed. *The Collector's Encyclopedia of Depression Glass*, 9th Edition. Paducah, KY: Collector Books, 1990.

Gibbs, P.J. *Black Collectibles: Sold In America*. Paducah, KY: Collector Books, 1987.

Gross, Leslie. *Housewives' Guide to Antiques*. New York, NY: Exposition Press Inc., 1959.

Grotz, George. *The Current Antique Furniture Style and Price Guide with Decorative Accessories*. New York, NY: Doubleday, 1979.

Hailey, Alex. *Roots: The Saga of An American Family*. New York: Doubleday & Company, 1976.

Hamilton, Charles. *Auction Madness: An Uncensored Look Behind the Velvet Drapes of the Great Auction Houses*. New York, NY: Everest House, 1981.

Huxford, Sharon and Bob, ed. *Schroeder's Antiques Price Guide*, 9th Edition. Paducah, KY: Collector Books, 1991.

Jenkins, Emyl. *The Appraisal Book: Identifying, Understanding, and Valuing Your Treasures*. New York, NY: Crown Trade Paperbacks, 1995.

Johnson, Frances. *Collecting Antique Linens Lace & Needlework: Identification, restoration and Prices*. Radnor, PA: Wallace-Homestead Book Company, 1991.

Jordan, Charles J. *What to Save From the 80's: A Guide For Collectors.* New York, NY: Ballantine Books, 1986.

Kovel, Ralph M. and Terry H. *Dictionary of Marks Pottery and Porcelain,* New York, NY: Crown Publishers Inc., 1953.

Kyle Husfloen, ed. *Black Americana Price Guide: A Comprehensive, Illustrated Guide to African-American Collectibles of the 19th & 20th Centuries.* Dubuque, IA: Antique Trader Books, 1996.

LaFarge, Albert. *U.S. Flea Market Directory.* New York, NY: Avon Books, 1993.

Lyons, Mary E. *Stitching Stars: The Story Quilts of Harriet Powers.* New York, NY: Charles Scribner's, 1993.

Lyons, Mary E. *Master of Mahogany: Free Cabinet Maker, Thomas Day.* New York, NY: Charles Scribner's, 1996.

McCarthy, Nancy. *Antiques Across America.* New York, NY: Avon Books, 1997

Reno, Dawn E. *The Encyclopedia of Black Collectibles: A Value and Identification Guide.* Radnor, PA: Wallace-Homestead Book Company, 1996.

Roberts, Ralph. *Auction Action! A Survival Companion For Any Auction Goer.* PA: Tab Books Inc., 1986.

Rockmore, Cynthia and Julian. *The Country Auction Antique Book.* New York, NY: Hawthorne Books Inc., 1974.

Smith, Nancy. *Old Furniture: Understanding the Craftsman's Art.* Boston, MA: Little, Brown and Company, 1975.

Vlach, John Michael. *Afro-American Tradition in Decorative Arts.* Cleveland, OH: The Cleveland Museum of Art, 1978.

Vlach, John Michael. *Charleston, Blacksmith: Philip Simmons.* Athens, GA: The University of Georgia Press. 1981.

Wills, Geoffrey. *Practical Guide To Antique Collecting.* New York, NY: ARC Books Inc., 1961

Illustrated Glossary

A

Absolute Auction — An auction where all the merchandise is guaranteed to be offered and sold to the maximum bidder. There is no minimum bid (or reserve) on any of the merchandise.

Acanthus — The stylized foliage of the acanthus plant, used as a decorative motif on furniture, silver and china. The acanthus is evident in Chippendale, Victorian, and Empire furnishings.

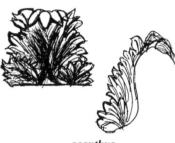

acanthus

Adams, Robert and James — Innovative furniture designers from Scotland who created light, graceful furniture styles from the neoclassic patterns that inspired Hepplewhite and Sheraton.

Adinkra — Textile produced by the people of Ghana and made with numerous patterns (or symbols) ranging from crescents to abstract forms. Each symbol carries its own significance and represents events of daily life.

Aesthetic Value — Having an appreciation for the artistic beauty of an item.

Age — A 'tool of the trade' used by auctioneers and appraisers to define the length of time an item has been in existence.

Art Nouveau lamp

Appraised Value — The written or oral value assigned to an item by a professional who specializes in defining the worth of antiques and collectibles.

Armoire — A tall cupboard or wardrobe, with front doors, used to store linens and garments.

Art Deco — Popular during the 1920s to the 1950s. Replaced the flowing lines of Art Nouveau with straight lines and spce-age designs. Plastic and chrome were added improvements to chairs, tables and other pieces of furniture.

Art glass — A general term used to describe decorative glassware, often of vivid colors and extravagant forms, widely produced in America between 1880 and 1910.

Art Nouveau — Literally means "new art" in French. A style of art and furniture design that began in the early 1890s and continued into 1930s. It is characterized by flowing lines, floral forms and entwined vines.

Arts and Crafts & Mission — A movement during the late 19th century in England (and America) to improve the quality of industrial art and design, largely through a return to the principles and methods of hand craftsmanship. Famous craftsmen during this period were Hubbard, Stickley and Frank Lloyd Wright.

ILLUSTRATED GLOSSARY 199

Antique — According to U.S. custom law, any object that is 100 years older and older.
Antiquing — The fun of shopping for and discovering antiques in non-traditional shopping arenas, like auctions, estate sales, thrift stores and flea markets.
Antique Automobile — Any car dating before 1930. Some judges also acknowledge cars that are twenty years old or more.
Apron — The horizontal cross where a piece of furniture connects with its legs. On a chair, it is the structure below and parallel to the seat.
Applique Quilt — A quilt where varying forms and patterns have been cut from contrasting colors of cloth and applied or "stitched" down onto a whole piece of material.
Appraised Value — The oral or written amount assigned to an item by a professional based on quality, workmanship, age, desirability and supply.

apron

Appreciate — An increase in the monetary worth of an item.
Architectural Antiques — Items such as crystal door knobs, stain glass windows, and brass hardware used in the construction and decoration of older homes, churches and other structures.
Artisan — A skilled craftsman who creates objects of beauty.
As is — A general warning at auctions and estate sales that merchandise may be damaged and will be sold with that understanding.
As is and Where Is — A phrase used by auctioneers to inform their buying clients that there is no guarantee on the condition of merchandise and that the buyer is responsible for removing any purchased merchandise from the auction premises.

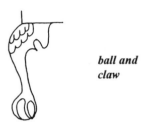

ball and claw

Auctioning — The act of selling merchandise at auction.
Auction block — The place where things are brought to be sold at auction. Unfortunately, African people were sold into slavery by this means.
Auctioneer — A licensed official who sells merchandise to the highest bidder at a public auction.

B

Ball foot — A round, turned foot with a flattened base at the sole. Popular in the 17th and early 18th centuries.
Ball and claw foot — A claw grasping a ball; used as footing on cabinets, tables, chairs by the Chinese and early Romans.

bracket foot

Barter — To trade goods and services.
Beading — Decoration used on furniture, that resemble a strand of beads.
Beveled mirror — Mirror where the glass is bent around the edges.
Bidder card — Official card used by auction goers to bid on merchandise.
Black figurals — Figurines or statues of African-Americans as decorative pieces.
Black light — A light used to detect needed repairs and damage in porcelain, glass and furniture.
Black Sambo — A little black boy.
Blue Ridge — Art pottery.
Bohemian glass — Ruby colored glass produced in Bohemia.
Bracket foot — The outer corner edge is straight and the inner edge is curved.
Brewster chair — A chair made during the colonial period with finials, spindles and a rush seat.
Brasses — The hardware used on furniture such as drawer pulls and plates.

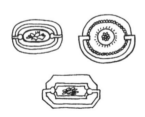

brasses

Buffet — A sideboard used for the storage of china, glassware, table linens, and flatware.
Bun feet — A slightly flattened round foot seen in Colonial style furniture.
Buyer's Premium — The amount added to the final selling price of merchandise bought at auction; usually between 3 - 15 percent.

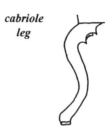

cabriole leg

C

Cabriole — A "S" curved leg terminating in a shaped foot.
Canopy — A top covering over a four-poster bed.
Caricature — A sketch of an individual that exaggerates their features, making them appear humorous.
Carnival glass — Iridescent glass appearing in marigold, green, blue, and aqua in color. It was originally given away at carnivals.
Cartouche — An ornament which looks like a scroll when it is unrolled.
Carver chair — A chair made during the colonial period similar to the Brewster chair and thought to have been brought over by Gov. John Carver on the Mayflower.
Ceramic — *See earthenware.*
Chenille spread - Made from cotton with tufted cords used for design.
Chest on Chest — *See highboy.*
China — Porcelain.
Chinese Chippendale — An intermingling of Chinese motifs and with Chippendale furniture.

cartouche

Chippendale, Thomas — An English cabinetmaker and furniture designer.
Christie's — A famous auction house based around the country.
Circa — Meaning "around the date of."
Club foot — A circular furniture foot that extends forward from the leg.
Collector — One who assembles or collects similar items from a number of sources.
Collectible — Any item collected or assembled by others.
Colonial Style — Furniture made while America was still an English colony. Includes William and Mary & Jacobean styles.
Commode — A low standing chest of drawers or cabinet.
Condition — The fitness of a particular item that may be excellent, good poor or fair.
Cornucopia — An festive fruit decoration used in Empire furniture.
Coverlet — A bed covering.

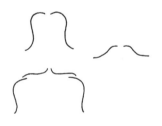

cyma curves

Crazing — A mosaic of fine cracks developing in the glaze of porcelain and pottery.
Curly Q's — Designs made from curling lines used to decorate furniture.
Cut glass — Glass with patterns cut in to it to form designs.
Cyma curve — An "S" or double curve used in furniture design.

cornucopia

D

Dahomey — An ancient coastal city and republic of West Africa. Now known as Benin. The Fon people of this region, along with the Fante of Ghana are known for using applique' techniques in their textiles. Colors are true to life and scenes are drawn from history, myths and everyday experiences. Typically, these vivid textiles create fashionable banners or flags.
Danescraft — Collectible jewelry.
Decorative art — Furniture and accessories enhanced by artistic embellishments that are used for decorating purposes.
Depreciation — To decrease in value.
Depression Glass — Mass produced cheap glass from the Depression Era, which comes in a variety of patterns and colors.
Disclaimer — To deny a connection to or responsibility for services rendered.
Disneyana — Collectible pieces of Disney characters and product trademarks.

drake feet

Doilies — Small crocheted piece of lace, used to adorn furniture.
Dovetail — An interlocking joint that connects two pieces of wood at right angles. Shapes like the tail of a dove are cut on the end of the board, then fitted into similar shaped cuts on the end of the other board. This technique creates strong and durable furniture.
Drake foot — A web or duck-looking foot used in furniture.
Durability — The lasting quality of an item.

E

Eastlake, Charles (1836-1906) — An English architect who popularized furniture with straight lines during the late Victorian period, from 1868 to 1890. His book, *Hints on Household Taste* was first published in 1868 and became a best seller in England and the United States.
Earthenware — A ceramic pottery that can be glazed or unglazed.
Eclectic — A blending of traditional styles with unusual combinations to create a new and interesting decor.
Empire Style — Massive, heavy carved furniture, that became popular following the reign of Napolean I. Empire furniture is characterized by elegant expressions of rich woods, with favored elements such as the acanthus, foliage, and paw feet.
Estate Auction — The auctioning of the entire contents of a home (or estate) through the auction method, rather than a tagged sale.
Estate Sale — A sale hosted and tgged by a professional where the entire contents of a home (or estate) is sold. *See tag sale.*
Egyptian Cotton — A very fine and soft cotton used to make linens and other textiles.
Eisenberg — Collectible jewelry.

F

Fair market value — The price at which a willing seller and willing buyer exchange merchandise without duress.
Four-poster — A bed with tall corner posts.
Fostoria — Pressed glassware made from 1887 to 1986 by the Fostoria Glass Company. Glass pieces include tableware, lamps, and figurines.
Fiesta — A line of solid bright colored dinnerware with concentric circles made by Homer Laughlin China Company of West Virginia.
Flea market — A central place where goods are bought, traded and sold.
Fret work — Ornament used to decorate furniture in which the lines meet and form different designs.
Functional value — The worth of an item based on its performance.

G

Galle', E'mile (died 1904) — Founder of a firm in Nancy, France in 1874 that produced pottery, enameled glassware, cameo glass and furniture. His cameo glass reflected the Art Noveau style.

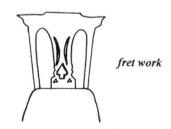

fret work

Gateleg table — An English drop-leaf table with 6 stationary legs and 2 additional legs which swing up like a gate to support the drop leaves.

Gateleg table

Gavel — The wooden, hammer-like instrument used by an auctioneer to officially preside over an auction.

Graining — Paint or stain applied to plain wood to imitate a grain.

Greek Revival Style - A revival of Greek architecture and furniture styles.

Goblet — A drinking vessel with a tall stem supporting a bowl.

H

Hand-blown glass — Glass made by hand blowing it into a mold.

Greek Ionic capital atop large column, popular during Greek Revival Style

Handel, Philip — Producer of fine art glass since 1885. Most pieces are marked "ANDEL" inside a large "H."

Homer Laughlin — Famous maker of ironstone tableware. Fiesta is a company creation that is highly collectible. Most pieces are marked "HLC" followed by a number.

Hard paste porcelain — A porcelain made of a mixture of rare clays including *kaolin* to form a hard paste. It originated in China.

Haviland — Dinnerware made of porcelain by the Haviland family company in Limoges, France. *See Limoges.*

highboy

Hepplewhite, George (died 1786)—English furniture designer whose style was characterized by simple, but elegant forms. He is best known for his shield-back chair.

Highboy — A two-section chest of drawers supported on high legs. *Also called a chest on chest.*

Hubbard, Elbert (1856-1915) — Founder of a publishing house, school and furniture company in the style of Arts and Crafts.

Hull — Art pottery dating back to 1905, most commonly marked "Hull USA".

Humidor — A container used to keep tobacco. Common among black collectibles.

humidor

Hutch table — A table with storage underneath the table.

I

Inlay — A design made by cutting various shapes into the wood and filling them in with contrasting material.
Industrial Revolution - Occurred around the 1820s when growth in industry fueled new machinery and mass produced items became common place, while hand-made items decreased in popularity.
Intrinsic value — The worth of an item based on emotional appeal.
Ironstone — Heavy pottery used to make tableware. A lot of the pieces were decorated in flow blue. Some pieces are unmarked.
Ironworking — The process of fusing wrought iron to form gates, fences, balconies, window grills and a host of other decorative arts. *See also Philip Simmons*

J

Jelly jars — Jars used to preserve home-made jelly.
Jeweler's loupe — A small magnifying glass usually set in an eyepiece.
Jumeau, Emile — Maker of expensive French dolls from 1876 to 1899. The first doll designer to produce dolls with sleep eyes

K

Kente cloth — A popular textile woven by the Fante people of Ghana; made by sewing strips of bright colored fabric together. Each color represent different aspects of social status and personal development.
Kwanzaa — Means "first fruits of the harvest" in Swahili and brings together the seven principles of unity, self-determination, collective work and responsibility, cooperative economics, purpose, creativity and faith to create a unique celebration, which runs from December 26 to New Year's Day.
Karat — The proportion of fine gold to fused metals used in an object or piece of jewelry.

L

Limoges — French porcelain made by the Haviland family in Limoges, France.
Lladro — Quality porcelain figurines and plates made in Spain since 1951. Highly collectible.
Lisner — Collectible jewelry.

M

Madame Alexander — An American doll company that was started in 1923. The company is still making dolls today.
Mahogany — A rich brown hardwood used in furniture making.
Mandate — An authoritative command to action.
Mantel — A shelf usually encasing a fireplace.
Maple — A hard light-colored wood used for floors and furniture.
Markdown — A reduction in the original price of merchandise.

original price of merchandise.
Marlborough leg - A square leg that ends in a block foot.
McCoy—Makers of kitchen art pottery, including a line of collectible cookie jars. The best known McCoy pieces were made after 1940 and may be marked "NMUSA." Newer designs are marked "McCoy".
Meissen - Excellent German porcelain that began in 1710. Since 1731, cross swords were used to mark their ware. Today "Meissen" is the simple marking.
Memorabilia — Items representing memorable events and lifestyles from a past time period.
Milk glass — Opaque white glass.
Mission Furniture — Late 19th century furniture that was designed as a result of the Arts and Crafts movement. The predominantly oak furniture was massive and plain.
Mortise and tenon — The joint created when a rectangular plug on one board fills a rectangular hole in another board.
Motif — The repetition of a particular design in a piece of furniture or art.

N

Nested table — Tables stacked upon each other in decreasing sizes.
Newel post — A wood post supporting the handrail at the bottom

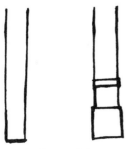

Marlborough leg

of the stairs.
Nippon — Japanese porcelain made for export to the United States. The finest quality Nippon is marked in green; the middle grade in blue and the lowest grade in a deep purplish red.

O

Oak — A yellowish to dark golden wood used to make furniture. Oak darkens as it ages.
Occupied Japan — Porcelain and pottery pieces made from 1945 to 1975 in Japan after World War II. These pieces are highly collectible.
Ornamental ironwork— Wrought iron that has been creatively fashioned into decorative art.
Ornate/Ornamental - exquisite decoration.

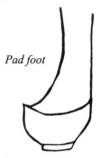

Pad foot

P

Pad Foot—Used in combination with the cabriole leg, this oval shaped furniture foot is flat on the top.
Parasol — A fancy, light umbrella used as a shield from the sun.
Particle board — Sawdust particles that have been pressed together to create wood.
Paste-board Miniature — A small, detailed replica or sample of a piece of furniture
Patchwork Quilt — Pieces of fabric sewn together to form patterns and designs. *See also applique quilt.*

Pattern glass — Glass that has been pressed together to form patterns and shapes.
Paw foot — A carved furniture foot used from the 17th century through the 19th century.

paw foot

Period — The specific time or era in which a furniture piece was made.
Pewter — tableware often used as underplates and resembles dull silver.
Phyfe, Duncan (1768-1854) — A well-known American furniture maker who created designs reflecting the Sheraton style and the Empire period.
Pie Safe — A tall, screened cabinet used to house and cool pastry.

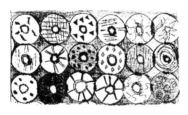
piece quilt

Piece-work Quilt — Joins together separate pieces of material in geometric patterns and borders.
Porcelain — Hard or soft it is used to make dinnerware, figurines and lamps. True porcelain is always translucent with a delicate look and feel.

Porcelain Trans Lucente — Clear, "see-through" porcelain
Pottery — Opaque clay earthenware.
Pressed Glass — Glass pressed into a mold to form various patterns. *See also pattern glass.*
Preview — The time allotted for potential buyers to view merchandise prior to an auction sale.
Provenance — The origin of a piece, where it was made or who owned it.

Q

Quatrefoil — Decorative ornament with four extensions. For example, a clover with four leaves or flower with four petals.

quatrefoil

Quilt — Pieces of fabrics sewn together with padding in between and top stitching that holds the entire material together.

R

Rarity — An item or thing not commonly available.
Red Wing — A line of art pottery from Red Wing, Minnesota that was designed in the 1920s. Earlier pieces produced as flower pots and jugs command high prices.

reeding

Illustrated Glossary 207

Reeding — Patterns in wood resembling thin parallel lines.
Replacement Value — The amount of money it will take to replace an older item in the present buying market.
Reproduction — An exact copy of an object or furnishing that also captures the details and quality of the original piece.
Reserve — A pre-determined minimum bid amount that will be accepted for an item at auction.
Rococo (Victorian) — Exquisite furniture featuring decorations of full curves and motifs of flowers, foliage and shells. Popular in the late 19th century.

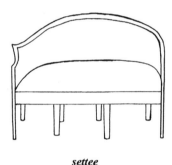

settee

Rookwood — Art pottery featuring animals, birds or people are highly collectible. The manufacturing of this pottery dates back to 1880 until 1967 in Cincinnati, Ohio. Pieces are marked with a "R" and "P" plack back-to-back and encircled by a flame.

S

Sankofa symbol

Sankofa — A symbolic pattern meaning "to return to fetch that which was lost and to move forward with it." Sankofa is one of the many patterns in the Adinkra cloth. Each symbol carries its own significance and represents events of daily life. This textile is deigned by the Akan people of Ghana. See *Adinkra*.
Sambo — A derogatory character used to depict a young black male.
Sarah Coventry — Collectible jewelry.
Secretary — A desk with top shelves and compartments enclosed by a door.
Semi-antique — Collectible items that are less than 100 years old; but highly collectible.
Semi-porcelain — Opaque porcelain with a hardened glaze that resembles hard-paste porcelain.
Serpentine fronts — A furniture front that looks like a wave, curving in the center and flattening out at the sides.
Settee—A small upholstered sofa.
Sevres — Fine, delicate porcelain that has been made in Sevres, France since the 18th century.
Shadow box frame — Picture frames with depth used to showcase large.
Shawnee — Pottery which resembles corn on the cob. Produced in Zaneville, Ohio until 1961.
Shell ornament — a motif resembling a seashell and used on furniture, porcelain and silver.

shell ornament

Sheraton, Thomas (1751-1806) — English furniture maker whose designs are characterized by

straight lines & graceful proportions.
Shield back chair — A Hepplewhite design where the back of a chair which resembles a shield.

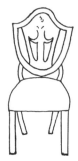
shield back chair

Shopping peg board — A black collectible used by cooks of yesteryear to keep up with shopping needs by putting pegs in categories (i.e. milk, eggs, rice, bread, etc.)
Sideboard — A dining room buffet or server that is commonly used to hold tableware.
Slat back chairs — A design where there are slats or straight horizontal pieces of wood across the back of a chair.
Sleigh bed — A bed made in the appearance of a sleigh in which the headboard and footboard are very high, forming outward like a scroll.

slat back chair

Slipper foot — A furniture foot which curves out like a slipper.

slipper foot

Snake foot — A foot which is made like a snake, used in furniture.
Sodium perborate — Whitening agent.
Soft paste porcelain — Porcelain made from soft paste and is not as durable or lasting as hard paste.
Spade foot— A furniture foot which is four sided and tapered.
Specialty auction— An auction where particular types of items are offered for sale.
Spiraling — A turning which spirals or curves.

spade foot

Spode — Porcelain and pottery manufacturers that date back to 1770. The company operates today as Royal Worchester Spode Ltd.
Staffordshire — Pottery and porcelain made in England. Figurines of dogs are very well known.
Sterling silver — A mixture of 925 parts silver to 75 parts cop-

per. It may be marked "925," "925/1000," "sterling." or "STG."
Steuben glass — Expensive art glass.
Steward — One who is actively concerned with and diligently watches over the inheritance of the family estate.
Stickley, Gustav (1857-1942) — A well-known maker of Mission furniture; which was inspired by the Arts and Crafts & Mission movement in England. Stickley furniture is signed and highly sought after by collectors.
Style — The fashion in which a piece of furniture is designed.
Supima cotton — A very fine and soft cotton used to make linens and other textiles.
Supply and demand — An economic law that states when supply is low, prices will be higher. When supply is abundant, demand will call for lower prices.
Swag — Ornament used to decorate furniture resembling a suspended rope covered with fruit, flowers and garlands.

swag

T

Tag sale — Formal, public sale where personal property (or merchandise) is tagged with a price by a professional host. See *estate sale*.
Tag sale conductor — A professional who host an estate sale and tags the merchandise for sale.
Tapestry — Heavy woven cloth that is decorative and reversible. Often used for wall hangings, upholstery and drapes.
Tea cakes — Thick cookies which look like little cakes.
Terms and conditions — Operating business procedures concerning the sale, purchase and removal of merchandise.
Textiles — fabric or cloth.
Tiffany, Louis Comfort (1848-1933) — Gifted designer of fine art glass. His father, Charles, was the founder of Tiffany & Company in New York City. He was well known for his *favrile* (iridescent) glass and stained glass designs.
Trade card — A small decorated card-piece that was circulated by 19th century merchants to advertise their shops and products.
Trefoil — Ornament design made up of three lobes used mostly in Gothic patterns.
Trendy crap — Faddish things in made in last 10-20 years.

trefoil

Trifari — Collectible jewelry.
Trifid foot — A furniture foot with three toes. See *web foot*.
Tripod table — A table supported by three legs.

U

Upholstery — Furniture covered with fabric, padding and cushions.

trifid foot

V

Value — That which is useful, important, or highly desired.

Valuation — The process of assessing the monetary worth of an item. Their are four basic assessment tools in valuation: fair market value, liquidation value, replacement value and appraised value.

Van Briggle pottery —Was started in Colorado Springs, Colorado, in 1901 by Artus Van Briggle. This pottery is heavy and distinctive and is found as vases, lamps, and other pieces. Markings prior to 1907 are inscribed as "Van Briggle." Until 1920, the date was dropped and "Colorado springs" was added.

Vendor — One who sells items of merchandise in a public market.

Veneer — A thin sheet of wood with a rich grain glued to another piece of plain or inferior quality wood.

Victorian — Furniture and accessories in a style influenced by English designers during the reign of Queen Victoria (1840-1901).

Vintage — An item that is old, but useable.

Warranty — A guarantee of the integrity of a product and the maker's (or seller's) responsibility for the repair or replacement of defective parts or problems.

Wash stand — A wooden stand with or without shelves that holds a bowl for washing.

Watts — A hand decorated pottery.

White work — White thread embroidered on a white background.

Web foot — A furniture foot with three toes. See *trifid foot* also.

Weiss — Collectible jewelry.

Welsh cupboard — A closet or cabinet with shelves for storing food and other kitchen items; associated with early colonists from Wales.

Will — To dispose of by a written legal document; to choose or decree.

Y

Yard sale — An informal sale of personal property that is held outside. *See garage sale*

Yo-Yo spread — Round pieces of colorful fabric (in different textures) that have been attached to make a spread or decorative covering.

Victorian table

W

Wares — Manufactured goods; articles of merchandise sold at a fair or market. *See also vendor*

INDEX

about...time Magazine, 22, 174
absolute auction, 117, 198
acanthus, ornamental, 67, 198
   illustration of, 198
Adams Brothers, 65, 198
Adinkri cloth, 74, 198
American art pottery, 94
   illustration of, 86
American Legacy, 174
Amos 'n Andy, *illustration of,* 104
Anchor Hocking, 81
antiques, furniture,
   African designs and, 74-75
   age of, 59
   appreciation of, 59-60
   appraisal of, 53-55
   architectural, 94
   antiquing, 60, 75
   condition of, 54
   cost of, 60
   decorating option, 60, 85-86
   definition of, 59, 198
   periods and styles of, 60-75
   provenance, 53-54
   rarity of, 55
   semi-antiques, 59
   why buy, 59
Antique Trader, 119
apron, furniture, 74, 199
   illustration of, 199
Architectural Digest, 88
Art Deco style furniture, 169
artisans,
   Clark, Chris, 13
   Day, Thomas, 26-29
   historical review of, 25-26
   modern references of, 183
   Potter, Dave the, 30-32
   Powers, Harriet, 32-36
   Simmons, Philip, 36-40
Art Nouveau style
   furniture, 70, 72
   illustration of, 72
Art Nouveau, decorative pieces
   illustration of, 72
Arts and Crafts & Mission
   style furniture, 73
   illustration of, 73

"as is," disclaimer of, 118, 160, 199
"as is, where is," disclaimer of, 118, 160, 199
auction, general, 115-133, 199
   absolute, 117, 198
   auction, estate sales, vs., 137-138
   block, 109, 199
   definition of, 109, 116
   the estate, 137-138
   job descriptions at, 131-132
   reserve of merchandise at, 117, 207
   personal property, 116
auction, buying at, 123-127
   bidder card, 130
   bidding process, 132-133
   classifieds, 116-118
   consignments, 121-122
   dishonesty with, 126-127
   finding sales, 116-121
   government disposal through, 120-121
   legal newspapers, 120
   reasons to buy, 115
   paying for items, 133
   private and public disposal through, 120-121
   retrieving items, 133
   potential competition, 124, 133
   the preview, 129-130
   trade publications, 119
   types of, 116
   strategies for, 123-127
   word of mouth, 119
auction, selling through, 121-122
   hiring an auctioneer, 144-146
   estate liquidation, 137-138
   homesite advantage,
auctioneering/auctioning,
   profession of, 110-114
   state licensing agencies for, 112-114, 192-194

ball and claw feet, *illustration of,* 64, 199
Bakelite, 74
Baker, Josephine, 106
barter, bartering, 160

beading, furniture, 200
bell jars, 22
Bennington pottery, 82
beveled mirror, 155, 200
bids/ bidding, 132-133
   silent, 141
   bidder card, 130
   bidder registration, 130
black collectibles, 99-106
   Amos 'n Andy illustration, 104
   Bull Durham illustration, 103
   commercial advertising, 102
   Darkie Toothpaste, illustration of, 105
   Diaper Dan illustration, 103
   dolls, 105
   F&F salt & pepper shakers illustration, 102
   figurals, 103
   Frederick Douglas, illustration of, 104
   history of, 99-101
   historical items, 101
   Jim Crow illustration, 101
   kitchen items, 101
   Little Brown Koko, illustration of, 105
   music memorabilia, 103
   new types of, illustration, 106
   paper collectibles, 104
   political memorabilia, sports memorabilia, 104-105
   toys and games, 102
   where to buy, 190
Black Enterprise, 88
black light, 167, 200
blacksmith, blacksmithing, 36-40
   See Philip Simmons
Blue Flow, 82
Blue Ridge, 82
Bohemian glass, 79-80
   illustration of, 80
Bond, Julian, 100
Books, collectible, *illustration of,* 88
bracket foot, 62, 64, 199
   illustration of, 64, 199
Brewster chair, 61
brasses, 200
   illustration of, 200
buyer's premium, 117, 130

cabbage patch, collectible, 95

cabriole leg, furniture, 62-63, 200
   illustration of, 200
Cambridge, 81
camel sofa, *illustration of, 157*
caricature, 99
carnival glass, 80, 200
   illustration of, 81
Capo-di-monte, 82
cartouche, ornamental, 70, 200
   illustration of, 200
cast iron skillet, 22
chairs, antiques,
   Brewster, 60
   Carver, 60
   ovals, 65
   interlocking, 65
   shield back, 65, 208
   slat back, 60, 208
Charles, Ray, *illustration of, 91*
chenille spread, 93, 200
Chinese Chippendale, 62
Chippendale style furniture, *illustration of, 64*
Chippendale, Thomas, 62
Christie's, auction house of, 53
collectibles, general, 77-97
   American art pottery, *82, 94*
   architectural, 94
   books, 88
   dolls, 90. 94
   Disneyana, 96
   embroidery, 93
   kitchenware, 89
   holiday items, 96
   legal documents, 97
   linens and textiles, 92
   office furniture, 89
   old photography, 94
   quilts, 93
   newspapers and magazines, 88
   smoking items, 96
   sterling silver, 95
   what to save, 87-92
   what to collect, 92-97
Colonial style furniture, 61
   illustration of,
Coro, 84
cornucopia, ornamental, 67, 201
   illustration of, 201
crazing, porcelain, 201
cyma curves, 62, 201
   illustration of,

INDEX   213

cut glass, 78
  illustration of, 51, 79
Dandrige, Dorothy, 166
Danescraft, 84
Dahomey, 33, 201
  illustration of quilt, 33
Day, Thomas,
  illustration of bed,
  childhood of, 26
  accomplishments, 26-29
  illustration of newel post, 29
  illustration of table, 27
Depression glass, 77-78
  illustration of, 78
Disney, collectibles, 96
disclaimer, 118
dovetails, 47, 48, 202
  illustration of, 47
drake feet, furniture, 62, 202
  illustration of, 202
Duncan Phyfe Style, 65,
  illustration of, 67

earthenware, 82, 202
Eastlake, Charles, 70
Eastlake, Victorian, 70-71
  illustration of, 71
Ebony, 88, 104
eclectic style, 85
Egyptian cotton, 49, 168
Eisenberg, 84
embroidery, collectible, 49, 83, 93
  description of, 49
  illustration of, 83
  old vs. new,
Emerge, 88
Empire style furniture, 67-68, 202
  illustrations of, 68
Elle, 169
Estate (tagged) sales, buying at, 137-148
  attending an, 140
  departing notes for, 142
  estate sale, auction, vs., 137-138
  finding sales, 139
  garage sales, 137
  pre-sales events, 139
  preparation prior to, 140
  reasons for, 138
  removing items from, 142
  submitting silent bids, 141

Essence, 88, 169

fair market value, 44, 202
favrile, glass, *illustration of, 72*
Fenton, 81
Fiesta, 82. 202
flea markets, buying at, 159-163
  bartering at, 160-161
  buying at, 161-162
  general operations of, 160-161
  history of, 159-160
  restrictions for, 160
  types of merchandise, 160
  vendor rapport, 161-62
flea market, selling at, 162-163
Fostoria, 81, 202
four-poster bed, Queen Anne, 16, 202
  illustration of, 139
French Jumeau dolls, collectible, 95
fretwork, furniture, 62, 64, 202
  illustration of, 202
furniture,
  antique periods and styles of, 60-75
  hand-made techniques of, 26-27
  old vs. new, 47
furniture feet, types of,
  ball and claw, 62, *64, 199*
  bear, 68
  bracket, 62, *64, 199*
  bun, 61
  club, 63
  drake, 62
  padded, 62, 63
  paw, animal, 68
  slippered, 62
  spade, *66*
  trifid, 62, *209*
  web, 210
furniture legs,
  cabriole, 62, *64, 199*
  Marlborough, 62, *64, 205*
  round tapered with reeding, 65, *66*
  spiraling turnings, *65*

Galle', E'mile, 70
garage sales, *137*
General Services Administration and auctions, 120

address listing of, 120-121
glass, types of,
  art, 79
  Bohemian, 80,
  carnival, 80, 200
  cut, 78, 79
  Depression, 77, 78, 201
  hand-blown, 51
  Handel, 79-80, 203
  old vs. new, 51
  pressed, 78-79, 206
  pattern, 206
  Tiffany, 80, 209
Gothic Style, Victorian, 70
  illustration of, 71
Greek Revival Style, 27, 28, 203
  illustration of,
Great American Women's
  Getaway, 23
goblets, silver, *illustration of,* 132
gold, markings of, 124, 168
Golden Oak, furniture, 71-72

Handel, Phillip, 79-80, 132, 203
Handel, *illustration of,* 80
hard paste porcelain, 203
Harper's Weekly, 88, 95
Haskell, Miriam, 84
Haviland, 82, 203
heir, 182
Heisey, 81
Hepplewhite, George, 65, 203
Hepplewhite, furniture, 65
  illustration of, 66
highboy, furniture, 203
  illustration of, 63, 203
historical riches, 14
  definition of, 14-15,
  artisans and crafts-
    people, 25-40
  material inheritance,
  oral traditions,
  special keepsakes,
Homer Laughlin, 82, 203
Hubbard, Elbert, 73, 203
Hull, 82, 203
humidor, 105
  illustration of, 204
humpback truck, antique,
  illustration of, 138

Imperial, 81
incised motif, 70
intrinsic value, 43
Ironstone, 82, 204
Jacobean style furniture, 61
jelly jars, 22, 204
Jet, 88
jeweler's loupe
  when to use, 124, 129, 140
  where to buy, 167
jewelry, collectible, 84
  illustration of, 46, 84,
Johnson Brothers, 82,

Kente cloth, 74, 204
Kwanzaa, celebration of, 175, 204

Life, 88, 95
  illustration of, 88
Limoges, 82
linens,
  care of, 54, 170
  collectible,
  how to shop for, 192, 54
  where to shop for, 49, 168
  old vs. new, 48-49
  types of,
Little Brown Koko, illustration of,
  105
Little Black Sambo, 104, 207

Lisner, 84
Lladro,
  description of, 82, 204
  illustration of, 81
Look, 88

Madame Alexander, collectible, 97, 204
magazines, collectible, 88, 154
mammy cookie jar, *illustration of,* 102
markdowns, 157, 204
Marlborough leg, furniture, 62, 205
  illustration of, 64, 205
material inheritance, 177
McCoy, porcelain, 50
  illustration of, 50
Meissen, porcelain, 50
memorabilia, general, 87-106
  black, 99-106
  fire and police, 92

INDEX   215

fishing, 96
media and entertainment, 90
political, 92
sports, 91
World Fair, 92
milk glass, 78
mink coat,
   illustration of, 153
Mission, Arts and Crafts, 73
   illustration of, 73
mortise and tenon, 27, 205
motifs,
   African, 74-75
   definition of, 205
   incised,
music box, antique, *illustration of, 97*
National Auctioneer Association, 111
National Geographic, 88
Negro Baseball League, 91,
   where to buy items, 190
newel post, 29, 205
   illustration of, 29
newspapers, collectible, 88, 95
Newsweek, 88
Nippon, 50
   illustration of, 50
Occupied Japan, 82
   illustration of, 145, 205
Old photography, collectible, 94, 104
   illustrations of, 94
oral traditions, 176
ornamental iron work, 36-40
   See Philip Simmons
Oriental rug, 153
   how to buy, 152-153
   illustration of, 153

Pairpoint, 81
paintings
   oil illustration, 155
   canvas illustration, 158
panel construction, 27
parasols, 22
particle board, 47-48
paste board miniatures, 28
paw foot, furniture, 68, *206*
   illustration of, 206
pearls, authenticity of, 124, 168
Periods, furniture, 60-75

Art Deco, 73-74
Art Nouveau, 70, 72
Arts & Crafts & Mission, 73
Chippendale, 62, 64
Colonial, 61
Duncan Phyfe, 65, 67
Empire, 67-68
Golden Oak, 71
Hepplewhite, 65-66
Queen Anne, 62-63
Sheraton, 65, 67
Victorian, general, 69-71
   characteristics of, 70
Victorian Eastlake, 70-71
Victorian Gothic, 70-71
Victorian Rococo, 70-71
Victorian Renaissance, 70-71
piece-work quilt, 93, 206
   illustration of, 206
pie safe, *85, 206*
pitcher & bowl set, English
   illustration of, 156
pocket knives, illustration of, 96
porcelain, 81
   manufacturers, 81-82
   illustrations of, 81, 50,
   old vs. new, 49-50
   semi, 82
   trans lucente, 81
pot belly stove, 22
Potter, Dave the, 30-32
   pottery illustration of, 31
pottery, 82
   old vs. new, 49-50
   types and manufacturers, 82
Powers, Harriet, 32-36
   description of 1886 quilt, 32
   description of 1898 quilt, 32
   illustration of 1898 quilt, 34
provenance, general, 53
   Jackie Onaasis, 53
   Princess Diana, 53-54
pure black skillet, 22

quatrefoil, ornamental, 70, 206
   illustration of, 206
Queen Anne style furniture, 62
   illustration of, 63
quilt,
   applique, 33.35
   Bible, 32-33
   Dahomey, 33

historical insights, 168
illustration of, 34, 206
pictorial, 32
pieced, 93, 206
see Harriet Powers,32-36
stitching qualities, 168-169
rarity, 55, 206
Red Wing pottery, 49
reeding, furniture, 66, 206
illustration of, 206
replacement value,
reproductions, 61, 62, 65, 70
reserve, auction, 117
ringmen, general, 131
Robb Report, The, 169
Rococo, Victorian, 70-71
illustrations of, 71
room divider, furniture,
illustration of,
Rookwood pottery, 94
Roots, 176-177

Salt & pepper shaker,
collectible, 101
illustration of, 102
Sankofa, 14, 20, 24, 29, 101, 207
illustration of, 207
Sarah Coventry, 84
Schroeder's Price Guide, 129,134, 167,
scriptural heritage, 176
secretary, furniture, 64, 207
illustration of, 64
semi-antique, 59, 207
semi-porcelain, 82
serpentine fronts, 65, 207
Serves, 50
Sepia,
Settee, furniture, 20, 207
illustration of, 207
Sewing items, collectible, 93
shadow box frame, 93,207
Shawnee, 49, 94, 207
shell, ornamental, 62, 207
illustration of, 63, 207
Sheration style furniture,
illustration of,
shield back chair, 65, 208
illustration of, 66, 208
shopping peg boards, 101
sideboard, 65, 208
illustration of, 66, 144

Signs, various,
Bull Durham, 103
Jim Crow, 101
Old motor oil, 46
silent bid, 141
Simmons, Philip, 36-40
national awards by, 38-39
illustration of, 37
Snake Gate, *illustration of,* 38
slipper foot, furniture, 62, 208
illustration of, 208
silver, sterling, 84, 95, 168
illustrations of, 72, 94
slat back chair, 61, 208
illustration of, 208
sodium perborate, 54, 170
spade foot, furniture, 65
illustration of, 66
spiraling turnings,
Spode, 82
Staffordshire, 82
Star Trek, 95
Star Wars, 95
steward,
Steuben, 81, 209
Stickley, furniture, 73
Stickley, Gustav, 209
Styles, furniture, 60-75
Art Deco, 73-74
Art Nouveau, 70, 72
Arts and Crafts & Mission, 73
Colonial, 61
Chippendale, 62, 64
Ducan Phyfe, 65
Empire, 67-68
Hepplewhite, 65, 66
Golden Oak,71
Queen Anne, 62-63
Sheraton, 65, 67
Victorian, general, 70-71
Victorian, characteristics of, 70-71
Victorian Eastlake, 70-71
Victorian Gothic, 70-71
Victorian Renaissance, 70-71
Supima cotton, *49, 168*
supply and demand, 55, 209
swag, ornamental, 209
illustration of, 62, 209

tag sale, 137-142, 209
conductor/host,

description of, 209, 137
tapestry, 14, 209
teacakes, 22, 209
textiles, 48, 92, 209
thrift stores,
  description of, 151-152
  exchanges and returns
    at, 156-157
  finding stores, 152
  general warnings
    about, 152-158
  how to shop at, 155-156
  markdowns, 157
  pricing concerns, 157-158
  retail research, 152-153
  what to look for, 154
  when to go, 153
Tiffany, art glass of, 80
  illustration of, 72,198
Tiffany, Louis Comfort, 80, 209
tiger oak, quarter sawn, 73
  illustration of, 141
Time, 88
trendy crap, 51
trefoil, ornamental, 70, 209
  illustration of, 209
toys, collectibles, 90, 96, 102
tricks of the trade, appraisal, 53-55
  age, 54-55,
  condition, 54
  rarity, 55
  provenance, 53-54
  supply and demand, 55
Trifari, 84
trifid foot, furniture, 62, 209
  Also drake foot
  illustration of, 209

upholstery, 65, 85
urn, 65

value, 43-52, 210
  aesthetic, 43
  definition of, 43-44
  appraised, 44
  enemy of, 51-52
  fair market, 44
  functional, 43
  intrinsic, 43
  liquidation, 44
  replacement, 44
valuation, tool of, 44

Van Briggle pottery, 94, 210
vendor, 159-163, 210
  selling merchandise,162-163
Victorian style furniture, 69-71
  illustration of, 69, 7⁻

Walker, Madam, C.J., 97
  certificate illustration, 97
Warman's Price Guide, 134, 156,
  167,
Wash stand, Black Italian, 142, 210
  illustration of,
Washington, Booker T.,158
  illustration of, 158
Watts, 49, 94
Weiss, 84
Weller, 94
will, 177
William and Mary, furniture, 61
Wiz, 84
wrought iron,
  See Philip Simmons,
Wright, Frank Lloyd, 73

yard sale, 137, 210
  See garage sales
yoyo spread, *illustration of,* 49

MEET THE AUTHORS

LaCheryl Cillie is engaged in an extraordinary search — uncovering rare finds, ageless antiques, and precious pieces from the past. She is involved in the business of auctions, where a public sale of property or items of merchandise are sold to the highest bidder. LaCheryl is the *only* licensed African-American auctioneer in the state of Alabama. With great strength and authority, she calls a public sale to order and sets the groundwork for how items can be purchased. When the word "Sold!" is uttered from her lips and the auction gavel sounds, no disputing words can follow.

In 1993, LaCheryl started her own estate sale business, Premiere Estate Services. Two years later, she attended the World Wide College of Auctioneering in Mason City, Iowa. LaCheryl has completed graduate studies in decorative and fine arts for the first 400 years of this country at the University of Montevallo, in Montevallo, Alabama. As a certified personal property appraiser, she can assess the worth of antiques, collectibles, automobiles, business equipment, and general household items.

Also a registered pharmacist, LaCheryl works for a national drugstore chain. When she is not filling prescriptions, LaCheryl is using "rapid-fire auctioneer's chant" to help local and national organizations with their annual fundraisers. She has hosted auctions for: The American Heart Association, Jefferson County Medical Auxiliary, First Real Estate, Big Brothers-Big Sisters and many others.

Today, LaCheryl spends time organizing tagged (estate) sales, selling vintage jewelry, linens and purses, and speaking to various groups about auctions, collectibles, appraisals and thrift store shopping. She is also a frequent guest on local television talk shows.

From Darkness To Light is LaCheryl's first book. "I was prompted to write a book because I no longer want my community defined by what I call 'throw-away garbage and manufactured junk.' We like to buy items that glitter, but have no true worth. Even our children like to wear expensive tennis shoes, multiple gold rings and trendy hairdos to define themselves. Where is the *real* value in this? I have learned so much about items of value that I feel a responsibility to pass it on to others."

MEET THE AUTHORS

Yolanda White Powell is President of Creative Inspirations, Ltd., a public relations, publishing and promotions firms based in Birmingham, Alabama. As a seasoned writer and editor she has sold dozens of articles to several magazines and newspapers. Yolanda is also the author of several Bible study workbooks including, *In Love With The Son: A Women's Study On The Book of John* and over 50 devotional materials.

Prior to forming her own business, Yolanda worked as a Public Information Officer for a alcohol & drug prevention agency, performed the duties of Assistant Development Director & Fundraiser for several non-profit organizations, and served as a Communications Consultant to a host of small businesses and social service agencies.

Professionally, Yolanda has served as Contributing Editor for *Urban Family and about...time* magazines, writing thought-provoking exhortations on marriage relations, child-rearing, and family strengthening. As a journalist, she has covered assignments on "Removing Cultural Barriers to Home Ownership," "A Passionate Vision of Equality for the Disabled," and "Breaking the Conspiracy of Silence on Women's Health," along with a host of interviews and personal profiles.

During an extended stay in Syracuse, New York, Yolanda worked as a radio announcer for WSIV (1540) AM and hosted a weekly, 2-hour, Gospel music program entitled, "The Gospel Alive!" She is a gifted communicator who conducts *YouthSpeak!* workshops, teaching teens the foundational techniques of public speaking, voice development and dramatic oration in an interactive setting.

Creative Inspirations, Ltd. is a diverse communications company that develops creative copy and voice-over productions for radio commercials, prepares corporate newsletters and designs a line of greeting cards and other specialty items. *From Darkness To Light* is their first book title. "I felt personally called to take on this book project. The sharing of 'old knowledge' packaged in 'new ways' was personally challenging to me. The African-American family is in desperate need of practical ways to return to the spiritual foundations of our forefathers. I feel confident that *From Darkness To Light* will fortify these efforts and pave the way for many generations."

Book Order Form

- Fax orders to: (205) 520-0212
- Telephone orders: Call Toll Free 1-800-390-4742 (Pin Extension 92). Have Amex, Visa or MasterCard ready.
- E-mail orders to: mobetter2u@msn.com
- Mail Orders To: Creative Inspirations, P. O. Box 610296, Birmingham, Alabama 35261, USA

☐ Please send *From Darkness To Light* to me at the following address:

Name:_____

Address:_____

City:_____State:_____

Zip Code:_____Phone: ( )_____

The cost of the book is $16.95. Please add 8% for books shipped to Alabama addresses to cover sales tax.

For shipping and handling: Add $4.00 for the first book and $2.00 for each additional book.

Payment (check one):

☐ Personal Check ☐ AMEX [AMERICAN EXPRESS] ☐ Visa [VISA]

☐ MasterCard [MasterCard] ☐ Money Order

Card number:_____

Print Name On Card:_____

Expiration Date:_____

Signature:_____

Call *toll free* and order today!